DETERMINED TO
CHANGE

DETERMINED TO CHANGE

5 Leadership Essentials for
People-centered Change
in a Fast-paced World

Dr. Loubna Noureddin
and Suzie Hise

Published by Sage Publishing House

To contact the authors about speaking, workshops, or bulk orders of this book, visit www.mindmarket.com

ISBN (paperback): 979-8-9904628-0-9
ISBN (ebook): 979-8-9904628-1-6
ISBN (hardcover): 979-8-9904628-2-3

Editors: Madalyn Stone, David Aretha, and Darine Noureddine
Book design: Christy Day, Constellation Book Services

Library of Congress Control Number: 2024913019

Printed in the United States of America

For MA
I carry your heart with me
I carry it in my heart

"True leadership is not about being in charge.
It is about taking flight with a vision,
inspiring others to rise with you."

Contents

Inside Out

Change brings along a whole baggage of nuisance when it interrupts our lives. It overwhelms us when it's unexpected. It can be exciting at times, and still disruptive to what is familiar.

Over the last several years, we all became managers of change. Around the world, our reality was shaped by different global events, and what we believed to be in our control took a new form. Change can take us by surprise, and new stories take hold, waiting to be told.

Change is relentless. Whether it is navigating the economic uncertainties we face, embracing new technologies like AI, implementing new systems, change in organizational design, or managing merging remote teams, change drives us to adapt and lead others through uncertainty..

The change we are referring to in this book is your everyday change, the one that impacts your life at work and the quality of your life at home. It is about the constant demand on you and your team to drive more change, and your constant race to make it happen, survive through it, and thrive with it.

This book began with a simple premise. Workplace change initiatives are failing in staggering numbers. Productivity and efficiency are paying the cost of emotional drain. What used to be a busy workday has turned into *agonizing* hours of unproductive meetings.

There is a better way to manage uncertainty, overcome the silence of resignations, and make work experiences less draining on managers and teams. People do not resist change; on the contrary they anticipate it. What they resist is the lack of regard for their experiences during change.

The *Disruption Syndrome* is not ending. It is just the beginning, and your talent will carry the load. Yet through disruption, you can reengage in the meaning of work and life. Disruption can inspire collaboration, empathy, and a genuine interest in the human element during change.

By picking up this book, you have made a mindful choice to pause and rethink the way you manage change. Perhaps you recognize the signs of conflicting priorities, the missing links in change, or the hamster in the wheel, the relentless *addiction* to busyness and meetings. Change keeps coming with no end in sight, and perhaps you want to learn new ways to manage change and influence others to adapt to it, without the burnout and distress you experience and observe in others.

Make no doubt about it, there is revolution brewing—a serious need to evaluate the way we lead lasting change. Based on three decades of supporting organizations and their leaders, we begin with insights from research and experiences of people about why change fails. We then introduce a five-step model that inspires a people-centered approach to change. These five leadership essentials are time tested by our clients and can be immediately applied to your everyday work and life.

We offer proven strategies and success stories of leaders who re-claimed their focus and re-aligned their teams to *make change work*, for a change. We offer you five leadership essentials to unlock the human potential during change. We invite you to take this journey with us. Whether you are implementing a new system, adding a new business unit, merging functions, or centralizing your IT team, change may fail during takeoff.

Books on change are abundant. In fact, you have a generous number of concepts and tools for navigating change. So why is this book any different? We offer you five *simple* leadership essentials that can elevate your influence during uncertainty. These tools are often forgotten because we are busy, and busyness is underrated. You are capable of driving people-centered change, we have no doubt about it. We offer ways for you to rise above the busyness and the shadow of overwhelming priorities.

When you build teams that are *determined to change*, you get lasting results. You inspire people to embrace new technologies, behaviors, and processes with a renewed sense of commitment, and that determination will shape your roadmap for success. We offer you practices that are people-centered and relevant during uncertainty and constant disruption. Are you ready?

Tell me what you really think.
I'd rather have a root canal.

Why Focus on Change?

"The only constant in life is change"
~HERACLITUS

Our experiences with change have been quite impressive over the last four years. The change we are referring to is your everyday change, the one that impacts your life at work and the quality of your life at home. It is about the constant change, the one that keeps coming your way, and your constant race to make it happen, survive through it, and thrive with it.

So What Makes People-Centered Change Important?

Change is disruptive. The past four years have been quite turbulent. Artificial intelligence, environmental disasters, unstoppable storms, stronger heat waves, strange illnesses, increased violence, political divide, and viral storms. Six in ten women, and five in ten men, have experienced at least one *trauma* in their life. Anxiety and depression are skyrocketing in our communities. Our decision-making and everyday thinking have been distorted by highly demanding to-do lists. Who would have imagined us talking about a pandemic of anxiety, immense loneliness, and horrific war crimes?

Change is failing. There is too much happening at one time. Your priority list keeps growing and you get to work with no idea about what challenge to tackle. Then, your boss shares his excitement about this new opportunity, your employee tells you she works in a hostile environment, and your son calls to tell he is in the principal's office. *Goodbye, list.* Suddenly, everything else becomes a priority. Get this: The resulting *physiological response* to constant, demanding priorities has been reported as similar to the symptoms of PTSD. It *endangers* your sense of well-being and *derails* the quality of decisions you make in your life.

Change takes time and effort. Parents across all sectors have taken on more household responsibilities while their endless projects at work have not faltered. Take Simone, for example, who works as a VP of Marketing in a global, not-for-profit organization. I asked her how she balances her life and work, and she said, "I go home every single day in time to make dinner, put my kids to bed, and then back to work with my laptop until midnight. It is my only time to catch up on emails because I'm in meetings all day." Simone is highly committed to her work and is really worried about disappointing her boss. She works every day of the week, until midnight. She is depleted and exhausted and continues to neglect her personal well-being. She needs her job to pay for her kid's college. During our conversation, Simone recognized her pattern and her pathway to burnout. She recognized that her work patterns were causing her distress and the constant sense of overwhelm. She also realized that she was modeling the wrong behaviors for her two teenagers. She acknowledged how near she was to burnout and decided to stop working late at night. Instead, she blocked out time during the day to focus on what is important, rather than urgent.

It is our reality. Change continues to catch us by surprise. No matter how well you plan or control your goals, you come face to face with complex situations without notice. Your attention is in high demand. The truth is you are living in *constant* multitasking mode and your *attention* span has significantly decreased over the past ten years. A study led by Microsoft Canada concluded that tech devices have decreased our attention span from twelve seconds to eight. You are witnessing a pandemic of *persistent* distractions and *instant* gratification. You get distracted, and just-in-time decisions may lead to reactive thinking and decision-making.

How Do You Typically Handle Change?

You run with it. You walk a fine line between tending to your leader's expectations while playing the "I got this" role with your team. You recognize the importance of bringing your team together to talk things out, and you may let that slip when you are busy with putting out fires. You know why it is important to get buy-in from your people, but urgency *trumps* proactive thinking when you are chasing crisis. You make that fire your priority, ready or not.

> Approximately 50 to 70 percent of organizational change initiatives fail.

You avoid it. More than 50 percent of people experience discomfort when dealing with constant change. You keep hoping the change goes away on its own. Your frontline teams joke about *the flavor of the month* when they hear of another change coming down the pipe. Only 33 percent of your workforce is engaged based on the most recent survey by McKinsey. The same goes for change. Approximately 50 to 70 percent of change initiatives fail in your organization. Communication is the culprit in most of them. Take, for example, your coworker, Lisa. Her manager invites her to brainstorm his super idea for the future of the department. Instead of scheduling a meeting with her boss, Lisa, true to her nature, prefers to avoid confrontation. She likes to think on her own and decides to send him a 23-page report instead, proving why his idea is doomed to fail. A pattern of avoiding conflict may increase the gap of conflict. Quiet quitting is motivated by *avoidance*. Coaching Lisa on how to manage conflict and present her ideas with confidence is essential to her success.

You freeze. Fear of failure during change can cause some of us to shut down. When Jamal, the chief medical officer of a global healthcare system, was asked to change gears, and to move out of the territory he had been working on diligently for a year, he experienced freeze. The CEO challenged him to lead a completely new territory, unknown to him, and for which he was ill-prepared. "I froze," Jamal told me. "I felt paralyzed. I could not move, think, eat, or sleep." Change can be difficult. The fear of failure can be debilitating. Another side of freeze is *stalling*—a time-honored practice of waiting for senior management to forget their idea in the first place.

You burn out. While many of us choose to be silent, some prefer to be bold and share without thinking. Research informs us that letting something simmer can lead to a worse situation, including resentment, guilt, stress, or burnout. When you suppress how you feel, you become more defensive or excessively quiet. Silence does not stop the physiological stress you carry as you move from one difficult situation to another. You burn out. Most managers are quite surprised or disappointed when their best person asks for a leave due to burnout—a warning sign that you may dismiss in high-demanding times.

We Are Lost in Transition

A small number of fortunate people thrive in managing crisis after crisis. Most of us don't. When everything is a priority, you lose sight of what truly matters. You don't have the luxury of being intentional about how you spend your time. You are busy handling the multitude of expectations, and that leaves no room to pause, reflect, and reengage in what matters. You live in a world where everything is a priority, and nothing is taken off the table. You feel pulled in different directions and pressed to do more with less. You become addicted to the urgent and get carried away in the wave of over-achieving.

We feel powerless. When things are difficult, we look for our organization to take care of us. When people we look up to fail to do so, we develop a sense of betrayal and disappointment that makes our experience painful. You feel alone, and the disconnect can impact your mental, physical, and collective health. You lose your drive and become disenchanted with new change. You decline any interest in connecting the dots and creating meaningful exchanges.

We are disillusioned. Our work with hundreds of managers informs us that you expect change; it is part of the job description. In fact, you anticipate it. What you resist is the lack of regard for your experience during change. Abrupt layoffs, mergers, acquisitions, and the consistent drive to do "more with less" can leave you feeling worthless. *I am just a number.* You feel that you must choose between being honest and being compliant. You stop saying "No" because you fear disappointing others or you fear career suicide, and the stress begins to eat your soul.

Our Super-Courageous Promise to You

We have been researching change and coaching leaders for over three decades. We have seen the shift in the workplace and the sense of resignation with constant change. We strongly believe that you deserve to find meaning at work. We believe that transformational change is possible, and your ability to master change will impact your circle of influence, your team, your organization, and your community. When you inspire others to be *determined* to change, they will find the resources they need to make it happen. They *own* the results with you. We promise that you will begin to manage the uncertainty during change with less stress, less resistance, and more resilience.

Our invitation to you is to elevate your leadership, connect to your life purpose, and inspire humanity in everything you do. We want you to reclaim your identity and to make change work for a change by paying attention to the drivers of the people side of change. Sixty percent of new managers *fail* within 24 months. Fifty to 70 percent of executives *fail* within 18 months. Think about the impact of these setbacks on you and your bottom line. We extend to you a promise that goes beyond mere rhetoric—an ambitious commitment to provide you with a diverse array of essential guidelines and tools. Equally vital is our emphasis on behaviors that inspire the heart and create momentum for people to want to make change happen.

Our exploration is not passive, nor imaginary. Through a fusion of theory, research, and practical exercises, we uncover insights gained from research and real-life work. Our commitment is to empower you with actionable insights that will resonate in your daily work. Our stories will help you recognize how teams drive lasting change. You will navigate the constant sense of overwhelm and drive decisions that enable your team to have a voice during change. We believe that the results will show up in four ways.

1. Improve your well-being. You cannot give what you do not have. You and the people around you have so much in common, yet most of the time, you struggle in silence. You want to look your best for your family, your employees, your managers, and your customers, yet you do not connect the dots when you have no energy to get out of bed. You hide your frustrations and pains well. You think you know what you want, and yet what you really want may not be that obvious, even to yourself. You want peace, yet you choose war with yourself and the people you care about. Peace happens when you align your values and beliefs to how you behave. The more you are aware of your hidden resistance, the more balance you will feel in your interactions with others.

Notice what you are tolerating and fix it. Don't let it eat your determination for breakfast. I worked for a toxic boss who was damn good at poking holes in everything I did. *Everything.* He even questioned why we planned monthly diversity days in the cafeteria. I tolerated his toxicity for six years. My wakeup call came from a child. My six-year-old niece told me, "I am worried about you, Auntie. I don't want you to get sick." Dima had more insight into my tolerations than I did.

Peace happens when you align your values and beliefs to how you behave.

2. Expand your influence. You want peace, yet you may be tolerating conflict with yourself and others. We tend to waste too much time focusing on our differences, not our common needs. You want the best for your organization, yet you avoid difficult conversations. When you are determined to make a difference, when you believe that you can contribute to a better workplace, the shift starts to happen.

When you lead change through a people-centered lens, you elevate your relationships and experiences with others. You become more transparent, authentic, and empowered to be yourself. You become determined to design *human moments* that build your momentum and inspire others to commit to change. When you protect the integrity of others, no matter their level of expertise or experience, you begin to surround yourself with people who care about you and about your success. You become a beacon of humanity, dignity, and integrity in the workplace.

3. Advance Your organization. Fifty to 70 percent of change initiatives fail in the US and the globe. Fifty to 70 percent! Big projects fail at an astonishing rate. It translates to billions of dollars in loss. A recent study by KPMG revealed that 70 percent of organizations have experienced one big project failure due to poor project selection. This monetary loss also hijacks employee morale and impedes organizational growth. Take for example the implementation of an electronic medical record in a healthcare system. This complicated long-term project is developed by a series of teams working along parallel tracks. Managers fail to anticipate *everything* that may fall through the cracks. One team works on creating templates, another team manages provider needs, and a third team works on IT analytics and training. Either team may fail to anticipate provider resistance or the complexity of certain specialties and patient population. These projects take longer than anticipated and consume tremendous resources over months and even years. Constant failures can demoralize employees. Elena, a middle manager at a large pharmaceutical company, told us, "I've been on dozens of project teams in my career, and I've never actually seen one project fully produce a result."

4. Bring back hope to your community. Children of today are the influencers of tomorrow. When we feel empowered, connected, and committed, our families feel it too. When we are overwhelmed, our actions become our children's lesson. Inspire our future influencers to be the change they want to see in the world.

Determined to change is an invitation to empowering others to find meaning during change. Inspire people to become your drivers of change. Recognize your power and decide *what* you will commit to and *how* you will influence it. Making change after change is easy; sustaining the change is not.

This book is divided into three parts. The first part explores the main causes of failure of change in organizations based on over a decade of research. The second part introduces five leadership essentials that drive people-centered change when stakes are high. The third part provides you with a change leadership competency model to guide the development of leaders and high-potential teams during relentless change.

The book ends with a summary of the 5C Model; a key anchor to our people-centered methodology. The 5C Model is seamlessly woven into chapters three through seven. It serves as a guiding framework and offers you a practical approach to navigating the complexities of change using people-centered strategies. It encapsulates the five leadership essentials and offers a practical toolkit for immediate application.

Our intent is to support your leadership journey during highly demanding times. We trust that you are capable, willing, and determined to take conscientious steps to reclaim humanity during uncertainty. We wish for you to live life with more compassion for self and others, more determination, and more fulfillment.

How we feel at work impacts how we parent at home, how we relate to our family, how we impact our teams, and how we influence our community.

Morale is worse than we thought. We need a quick fix.
How about cookies for all the units?

The Crash Happens During Takeoff

"If I had an hour to solve a problem, I'd spend
55 minutes thinking about the problem and
5 minutes thinking about solutions."

~ALBERT EINSTEIN

Most Change Efforts Fail During Takeoff

There are many reasons why big projects fail. Over a decade of research on workplace change reveals that most crashes happen *before* takeoff. According to KPMG, 70 percent of organizations have experienced at least one project failure in the previous 12 months.

Geneca, a software development company, surveyed 600 business executives who shared the story of *high-stake* projects doomed from the onset. Just like planes, the crash leads to misses before *takeoff.* Contrary to planes, the crash may not be felt upon impact. It may be years before the shattered glass and metal hit the ground, and the loss is reflected much later in financial reports. Make no mistake about it, whether immediate or delayed, these losses are significant to your bottom line.

How many change initiatives have you experienced at work that failed during takeoff?

Failure to launch happens. Competing priorities, cutting corners, ignoring red flags, rushed deadlines, overcommitment, and/or choosing the wrong project are among the reasons behind failed change. New leadership may change the direction of strategic initiatives with minimal interest in the history of the organization or the challenges that the frontline may have encountered in the past.

In general, when implementing change, managers believe that they provide a structured approach that invites clarity down the echelon. You invest and follow a proven change methodology to eliminate chaos and the unnecessary rework during change. There is another side to change that is not as emphasized—the people side. Failure to launch might be stalled by poor processes or tools for change, yet projects mostly fail to sustain due to the people side of change.

Failure during launch happens when expectations are not reasonable and goals are unattainable. Large-scale projects, across the globe, were doomed to fail from the start when top leaders did not take enough time to connect the dots and involve people from different levels of the organization from the onset. Missed connections are missed opportunities for buy-in. Failure to launch also happens in our workday, every day, when we react to what's right in front of us, without paying attention to what might be more important. To change how we manage change is a change initiative in itself.

Gartner, an information technology firm, estimated that 55 percent to 75 percent of all enterprise resource planning (ERP) projects fail. The implications are billions of dollars in lost sales and shareholder confidence.

Most plane crashes take place during takeoff. Organizational change is no different.

Take a moment to consider your experience with work-related change in the past two years. How many projects ended up in an expensive binder on a shelf? How many failed change efforts would you associate with poor *takeoff*? Do your peers joke about the *flavor of the month* when they refer to a new project coming down the pipe? Can you think of one change initiative happening right now that may be doomed to fail during takeoff?

The complexities of an ever-shifting global reality demand new and innovative ways to lead and manage change. Ambiguity is a magnifier of stress, and people are tired of drinking change from a firehose. They don't perform; they choke.

Recent workforce engagement scores tell the story of burnout and a deeper quest for meaning. Employees are not leaving the workforce; rather, they are questioning the *meaning* of work and the value of their personal and professional choices. Finding meaning is directly associated with making progress. We cannot continue to engage an entire workforce in constant change when resources are depleted. Instead, we must find ways to engage in meaningful dialogue that allows the team to collectively find meaning and inspire intention in the way we work and execute new change.

Most managers report feeling depleted from putting out fires all day long. Living in constant crisis mode is exhausting. You become reactive as you push through problems to solve at every hour of the day. Managers refer to the "roller-coaster effect"—the ups and downs and twists and turns that their teams experience from constant change. Right at the peak of a project, a senior leader introduces a new, more promising direction for change, spinning teams in a different direction. These changes demoralize employees, who experience lack of closure and a lost sense of accomplishment.

There are many reasons for failed change. In this chapter, we share seven most common gaps leading to *failure to launch*.

1. Misalignment

The disconnect among top leaders is one main reason for the failure to launch. Take for example the merger of three companies at Care Systems, a leading innovator in MSO and third-party administrative services that supports primary care physicians and specialists across North America. A joint venture with three other startups was quite promising for the strategic direction of the organization. Sustaining the Care Systems culture of compassion, pride, and connection were non-negotiable values for the CEO and his executive team. They unanimously agreed that *consistent* communication was a top priority to align people to their vision and to promote transparency across all levels of the organization. The joint venture caused significant fear among employees, and they voiced specific concerns about losing the special culture at Care Systems. While their executives were strongly committed to the culture, clashes started to emerge among new leadership team members. The threat of losing two key players on the original Care Systems team became a top concern, and the urgency to hold open communications with first-line teams took a side turn. Top-down communication became blurry, and the front-line team was less and less willing to report on technical challenges. They avoided conflict with their senior executive, who would snap when they shared concerns. To their surprise, their billing system crashed, causing millions of dollars in coding and billing delays.

The disconnect also happens when we have the right motive for change but miss the opportunity to connect the dots for those who matter. Mesha, head of nursing in the emergency room (ER), recognized the possibilities that the patient experience could have on her patient satisfaction score. Recently promoted, Mesha was too familiar with the concerns patients had about endless waiting times in the ER and the lack of communication from nurses in keeping them abreast of the next step in their clinical care. Mesha contacted her colleague for help and asked him to design a state-of-the-art animated video that would entice her team to buy in to the idea of managing patient expectations in the ER. "Our numbers are staggering, and I know without a doubt that they will commit to supporting me if we touch their hearts instead of giving them another set of policy changes," she explained.

Mesha was excited about building a course that touched the hearts of her team and reminded them of the reason they chose patient care. She had read our research and believed in the power of purpose. She invited a team of seasoned and new nurses to facilitate the conversation and provide training for staff. With her team's help, she came up with three animated avatars that symbolized the true essence of nursing care. The team loved the ideas they generated with the course designer and became excited about the prospect of impacting the patient experience and creating meaningful interactions. Mesha shared the exciting news with her lead physician, Jill. To her surprise, Jill was furious. She had no idea about the project and was concerned that the medical team had not been included. The program crashed before takeoff.

Despite great intentions, neglected people pieces can cause the crash to happen. Mesha had great intentions but, in her rush to make a difference, she undermined the authority of a key partner who needed to know prior to launch.

2. Lack of Trust

Organizational theorists Robert Blake and Jane Mouton examined NASA's findings on the human factors involved in airline accidents. NASA researchers placed cockpit crews—pilot copilot, and navigator—in flight simulators and tested them to see how they would respond during the crucial 30 to 45 seconds between the first sign of a potential accident and the exact moment it occurred. Their findings concluded that leaders are far more likely to make mistakes when they act on *too little information* than when they wait to learn more. In essence, the "know-it-all pilots" were quick to act on their *instincts* and made the wrong decisions more often than the pilots who *involved* their crew in problem-solving and decision-making.

Before choosing a course of action, pilots who solved the problem effectively created the space for *open exchanges* with their crew members and seemed to have a good rapport with the team. The findings also revealed that crew members who had regularly worked with the know-it-all pilots were *unwilling* to intervene, even when they had information that might save the plane. The know-it-all pilots nurtured a culture of *mistrust* and one-way communication. This lack of transparency in communication led to *serious errors* that might cause a plane to crash because of unresolved communication and respect issues.

During an emergency, pilots need to communicate not just by issuing commands but also by sharing information in the clearest and most transparent manner possible. Without that, they cannot be as creative or make course corrections effectively, and this often leads to business and ethical disasters. In this case, the know-it-all may disregard the knowledge of the team, which can result in a much more serious problem such as the loss of innocent lives.

3. Incomplete Information

When we hear of something happening at the top, we rely on informal ways of knowing to seek control or to feel safe. We feel safe when our story is complete. A complete story—even through the grapevine—feels better than not knowing. *Ambiguity* feeds fear and uncertainty during constant change. People will fill in the blanks for you when you don't. Our minds cannot rest until we have closure, a clear picture of what the end result is. If a movie ends with ambiguity, viewers go crazy contemplating the ending. Closure is essential to our well-being. We are hardwired to find the last pieces of the puzzle to complete the story. We cannot help but bring to light what we perceive as hidden.

The grapevine in organizations becomes rampant when transparency is scarce. Frontline staff may complete the story for you *automatically* when you do not share the full picture. When the story is incomplete, you can count on your team to complete it for you, with less accuracy. Misses in communication build gaps in operations. In a complex environment where change is rampant, stories run rampant, and a sense of overwhelm takes over. *When everything becomes urgent, nothing is.* Crisis after crisis feels like drinking water from a firehose.

The grapevine in organizations becomes rampant when transparency is scarce.

Confusion coupled with stress and frustration can lead to hiccups and unnecessary rework. Spending more time with your team is time-consuming, but it is critical to ensure a healthy takeoff. In many cases, the financial shortfall of missed deadlines is the result of *misused assumptions* prior to takeoff. It is in these moments that we need to create space for dialogue; to listen and inject a renewed sense of purpose, optimism, and encouragement. These moments put people at the center of your change effort and help your team recognize meaning during change.

The way we manage change calls for a reboot. There is a need to elevate our leadership and promote people-centered solutions during complex change. According to a recent Microsoft work study, only 12 percent of CEOs report having full confidence in their team to lead change. Managers also report less confidence in their ability to manage the constant demands at work and at home. We are caught in a tsunami of change where people are reshuffling the concept of work and seeking work environments that support their autonomy, while global work studies call for the immediate development of authentic leaders and the reskilling of the workforce.

The way we manage change can no longer be viewed as a one-time intervention; rather, it is an essential management strategy that supports the long-term survival of your organization.

4. Abandonment

We want the best for our teams, and yet most people share stories of abandonment during change—a moment in time when they realize that they are just a number. They feel abandoned when their ideas or concerns about the change are ignored. When people with reflective and thoughtful workstyles feel unheard, they shut down, literally. They choose to stay quiet and "just do the job."

Dan Price defeated abandonment when one of his employees shared her personal struggles as he was ready to announce the biggest win in the history of Gravity Payments. Dan Price is an American business executive, the cofounder and chief executive officer of a credit card processing company, Gravity Payments. Dan made headlines around the world when he decided to increase his entire team's minimum wage to $70,000. He was talking to one of his employees, a single mom, who shared her struggle to make ends meet. Dan was passionate about leading through meaningful purpose, so he slashed his $1 million salary in order to bring equitable pay for his team. While many praised the decision as a bold step toward combating income inequality, others vilified Dan as a radical socialist whose "experiment" was doomed to fail.

Behind the headlines and controversy about his plan is a much more personal story—a story of a CEO who realized he could no longer claim to be upholding the values of his company if he continued to gain millions while his employees received anything less than a living wage. How could he align growth to his company's purpose? How could he continue helping small businesses fulfill their mission if the people responsible for helping those businesses were struggling to meet their own basic needs?

Dan did not make the change alone. He embarked on this change alongside different levels of employees in his company. He made sure their voices were heard. He *overcommunicated* his listening. Today, over 17,000 businesses partner with Dan Price's business, Gravity, to help them save them millions in fees and hours of processing frustration. No hidden fees. No surprises. Meaning. Clarity. At a time when every company struggled to retain employees, Dan Price's company had *zero* turnover rate in 2020 and 2021 and 2022.

5. Superficial Compliance

When highly committed and capable leaders have a clear sense of the end in mind, they might get frustrated with the people side of change. They take the driver's seat with little tolerance for daily interventions, blocks to progress, or course correction from their teams. Rushing through change with less regard to operations breeds *superficial compliance*. Superficial compliance can derail your best laid plans. Angie, an SVP of operations in a biotech company, explained the concept of superficial compliance beautifully. "The CEO comes to the room, asks for progress, shares his ideas, asks if anyone has a problem with his recommendation. 'Tell me now! I don't want to hear it from people outside this room.' He stares at us impatiently. We all nod in silence, then he stands up and announces, 'End of meeting,'" Angie said.

What are signs of *superficial compliance*?

One sign is silence. How much silence do you notice in management meetings? When no one asks the difficult questions, that is a sign of superficial compliance. When your team chooses pleasing *over* speaking up, you are in the presence of superficial compliance. When you find yourself in an environment where opposing views are discouraged and conformance is rewarded, you are in the presence of superficial compliance. Superficial compliance works for you until takeoff.

Superficial compliance breeds *resistance*. We can demand compliance from our teams for only so long, and resistance can show up in unexpected ways. It prevents new ideas from permeating *up*. It drives your talent to *silence* or hand delivers them to the competition. When teams experience superficial compliance and they are encouraged to "deal with it," change begins to slow down or falter. People begin to shove errors under the rug to avoid conflict, retaliation, or intimidation.

Superficial compliance promotes fear, and fear gets in the way of creativity and trust. Fear drives our innate need for safety, not creativity. Fear blocks innovation as employees work relentlessly to hide mistakes, causing the crash to happen *unexpectedly*. Your frontline employees see, hear, and experience the problems you wish to solve. The way you communicate change has to make sense *to them*. For them to be committed to the project, they must be able to foresee how the change makes their jobs *easier*. The process must make the job easier *for them*. Your frontline staff can clearly see the tiny cracks that are less visible from the top.

You can fight superficial compliance. When you encourage open dialogue and messy conversations, you begin to promote psychological safety among team members who avoid conflict and thrive in harmony and stability. Empower your team to walk beside you. Reward honesty and integrity. Listen to what is not being said. Give your power to others so you inspire them to become determined to champion a healthy takeoff.

Silence happens when they give up on your listening.

Cultures that experience superficial compliance *mute* the very same experts they hire for their expertise. They recruit the best specialists in the field for their knowledge, and then disregard their advice when faced with tight deadlines. They want the experts to suspend their knowledge when it gets in the way of their drive for results. Thus, we substitute expertise for silence, and prefer conformity to valid contribution. Where superficial compliance resides, experts choose silence to protect their reputation or job security.

Boeing, an aircraft company that wanted to compete with Airbus' A320 Neo, reported over $20 billion in crisis-associated costs. Compelled to accelerate the development of its Boeing 737 Max, its top leaders opted to cut project time by 50 percent. They were also pressed to cut costs, which inevitably meant cutting corners. The tragic outcome, outlined in a congressional report, was two fatal crashes and the loss of 346 lives. The immeasurable damage to Boeing's reputation continues to unfold. Doing more with less is the core of efficiency. Yet, the question is: What corners are you willing to cut at times of turbulence?

Cultures that experience superficial compliance *mute* the very same experts they hire for their expertise.

6. The Purpose Gap

Organizational change models are abundant. These models offer comprehensive tools and guidelines to help managers implement change. You recognize the importance of aligning the vision for change to a clear purpose. You are aware of the significance of the projects you lead and can articulate the need for the new with conviction. The question is how much time do you block on your calendar to communicate the vision and assess progress?

There is a striking difference between how leaders perceive the impact of their communication during change and the reality that their teams experience. A recent study by McKinsey depicts a staggering difference between how executives connect to purpose versus how their frontline managers and employees do. While 85 percent of executives agree that they live their purpose through their everyday work, 85 percent of frontline managers are unsure or disagree that they live their purpose through the work they do. Leaders can clearly articulate how their daily work connects to a higher purpose. Frontline managers and employees do not. Figure 2.1 depicts the gap between executives and frontline managers and employees.

It is not the abstract language of vision and mission statements that drives purpose. It is the leader's influence and consistent connection to

Figure 2.1. The Purpose Gap

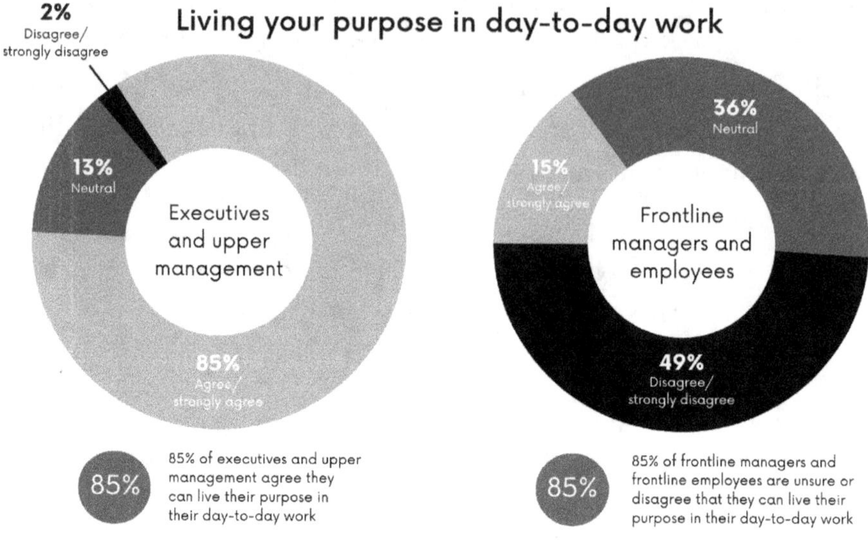

their teams that can reduce the purpose gap throughout the culture. Without purpose, the journey lacks drive. It seems impossible to do this when leaders are challenged to compete and get ahead of the game. An intentional investment in team culture can fuel organizational change to an unprecedented rate. When we take the time to explore the ripple effect of change and its impact on our teams, we accelerate their commitment to bottom-line results. The lack of regard for the experiences of people during change channels fear, disrespect, and a perceived loss of control. It leads to unnecessary resistance. Ambiguity stands in the way of progress, and the disconnect between expectations and reality may cause the crash.

Lack of clarity channels fear, resentment, and loss of control. It leads to unpredictable resistance.

7. Competing Priorities

In an ideal world, high-potential teams and culture champions work together to implement the vision for change. They recognize the value of strategic *alliances* and dedicate considerable time to create an *integrated* vision and process for change. Alignment is not a one-time event or a checklist on a reporting tool. It is intentional and deliberate. It requires time and planning. It is not a last-minute addition to the plan. It is a time-specific commitment to share the vision and strategic priorities for change.

When leaders compete for their favorite projects, misalignment shows up in overstretched budgets and resources. Competing projects, at the C-level, lead to competition among frontline teams for resources. Teams feel its effects when different functions struggle to meet their deadlines. As executives wrestle for time and attention, their support teams—IT, marketing, communications, training and quality, among others—operate in crisis mode through last-minute demands and urgent, time-sensitive deliverables. This leads to broken promises and missed deadlines. As a result, the information that they provide to executives may be compromised. Teams feel pressured to report positive outcomes, and ultimately they feel pressured to discount warning signs. They miss the opportunity to analyze minor errors, because bigger errors demand their attention. Lower levels of management may assume the top is aware of their challenges and mistakenly resent the chain of command for their lack of support. High-potential people on your team may resign themselves to silence, question the process, or quit.

Ronda, supervisor of material management at a biotech company, committed a costly yet avoidable error in procurement. Every team huddle became focused on avoiding the same error. "I was so embarrassed because my name was on everyone's mouth. Instead of working with me and my team to problem solve and identify the root cause, they instructed all team huddles to discuss the error." This seemed punitive and embarrassing to Ronda. To make things worse, they mandated training for all employees to ensure that the same error was not repeated. To prevent a costly mistake from happening again, the leadership team created more work and frustration among seasoned employees. Most found the training worthless and a waste of their time. This diversion was an attempt to check the box and avoid litigation. Ronda told me she was too embarrassed to stay and was leaving in a few weeks. She loved the organization, but the humiliation felt too personal. She admitted that she no longer reports minor mistakes and spends more time fixing issues *quietly* rather than sharing her insights with her manager.

Adecco Group's global survey of 14,800 employees in 2021 depicted that "the workforce has never felt more disconnected from the organization and leaders." This speaks to a lack of awareness about how teams view culture and the organization. Self-awareness, a core competency for effective leadership, when absent, can result in a *toxic culture* that discourages engagement, productivity, and the retention of top talent. A toxic culture is usually rife with indignities. Researchers are concerned that with advancing technologies, organizations may become less aware of the impact of their actions on their workforce.

People spend a major part of their time at work. In a disconnected culture, the threat to a worker's dignity shows up as mismanagement, overly long hours, bullying, and harassment. Women in particular experience a denial of their dignity through abusive communications and questions about their ability to manage their personal lives and work. To question their competence exacerbates the disconnect between leaders and their teams. This disconnect also occurs in how managers define and exercise their purpose at work and how they act on their values. If there is a *value gap* between leader and employee, it will be filled by anxiety and fear.

A good example of a value gap is the ongoing debate about the productivity of remote work. Working parents view remote work as a necessity for survival. The time spent commuting to work is considered a waste of time, an old way of thinking. Remote work, many leaders believe, stands against culture norms, team cohesion, and active engagement in culture. More importantly, remote workers feel pressured to prove their productivity at work. They spend more time proving their worth, rather than doing the job that matters to the bottom line. Avoiding conversations about the value gap with employees leads to resentment and disconnect. Employees may assume negative intent. They speculate about the lack of appreciation for their work or lack of empathy for their daily struggle to manage life and make ends meet.

In a 2022 study by the Conference Board, 55 percent of millennials, those workers born between 1981 and 1996, were questioned about what might be necessary to shift from the flexibility of remote work to coming back to the office. Some believed that creativity necessitates face-to-face interactions. The growing resistance continued to cause a gap between millennials and their colleagues who valued the workplace over remote work, especially baby boomers, born between 1946 and 1964, of whom only 36 percent questioned the move back to corporate offices. Emily Laber-Warren, a longtime science journalist and top editor at *Scientific American Mind*, *Women's Health*, and *Popular Science*, suggested that the 9-5 schedule should be the next pillar of work to fall. She stated that "30 percent of workers around the world surveyed last year said they would consider seeking a new job if their current employer required them to return to the office full time." Not surprisingly, most companies have incorporated the flexibility of remote work into their corporate cultures.

Dawna Ballard, a professor at the University of Texas, Austin suggested these simple culture tweaks:

- Scrap all but the most essential meetings.
- Don't expect remote workers to always be available.
- Focus on results, not start times.

I met with Marcia, a VP of marketing at a large tech system, who shared her disenchantment with what she said could have been a great opportunity. "I can manage consistent demands, but I have lost track of what makes sense because, in my organization, reactive thinking wins over systemic solutions." Her team is pulled in different directions, and their effort to make change purposefully is consumed with last-minute fixes. "I want to be proactive, but I find myself pushing more reactive work to my team, which causes frustration and resentment at me. They asked me who I identify as high risk for retention, and I told them all of my team is high risk!" Change fails during takeoff when conflicting priorities trump *strategic* alignment. Keeping up with deliverables becomes like shooting darts with our eyes closed, hoping one dart hits the target. Marcia's experience is not unique. It is an expected reaction to working in a crisis mode for too long. I facilitated a much needed conversation between Marcia and her manager. Together they agreed on a better way to manage expectations with less meetings and more focus on results.

> Change fails during take off when conflicting priorities trump strategic alignment.

When Everything Is a Priority

As we focus on a higher purpose and one vision for change, the letdowns of broken communication and conflicting priorities subside. You shift from a state of everything is a priority to focusing on what is *the* priority. Shogo Ikeuchi, the former CHRO of Recruit, a Japan-based company that owns job-focused websites such as Indeed and Glassdoor, has been quoted as saying that Recruit would never, ever, fund a project that delivered only financial returns because doing so would violate one of its three core principles: "Prioritize social values," "wow the world," and "bet on passion." Ikeuchi insisted that his leadership team find a balance between social value and profit so that their bigger vision for change became an adoption strategy. For over eight years, Recruit funded Study Sapuri, an online learning platform for students with the goal of addressing the country's educational inequities. He stated that Recruit funded projects that balanced their goals for growth with equal contribution to their core principles.

NeXt Elements is a top construction business development company. The CEO is known for his brilliance in the field and has been credited for creating family destinations in America. To be exact, 138 standard work initiatives were completed in 2015. Three years later, the CEO was interested in reporting his success journey with his new board of directors. I was standing in the executive conference room on the ninth floor to share my findings with the executive team. I had to report a not-so-glamorous reality. Out of 138 process improvement initiatives, only nineteen sustained.

The disbelief among the executive team shifted into discomfort, which turned into blame. The subtle threats by the CEO added to the loud finger-pointing in the room. I asked the team to take a pause and reflect on their team's culture throughout the change effort. I shared my observations and how the executive team might have contributed to the breakdowns in communication. "Can we take a moment to reflect on our behaviors, and share a perspective that is blame-free?" I asked.

The discussion that followed shifted from blame to a more meaningful exploration of resistance to change and lack of transparent reporting during change. Competing priorities, fear of failure, and negative assumptions about the benefits of the project were among the many reasons behind failure. The team decided to focus their efforts on three areas:

1. Clarity of purpose
2. Current narratives about the change
3. Connecting the dots for their teams

A significant number of new employees had joined the organization in the past year, and they had worked tirelessly with negative returns and consistent complaints from end users. What followed was a plan to hold open conversations with key functions at all levels of the organization. The vision and roadmap for success became more inclusive. Sustainable outcomes through a common purpose and a common narrative for change mitigated the lack of trust in the change process.

The leader's narrative supported by consistent actions drives progress.

When you communicate a clear purpose and connect it to clearly defined behaviors, you defy the gravity of *conflicting* priorities. You can then shift from a competitive silo mindset to a mutual purpose for change. Being intentional about creating connections and authentic relationships can shift the focus from a survival of the fittest to a focus on collaboration where a shared attention to results leads to higher levels of goals to a change process that promotes transparency, clarity, and safety.

Patty was a warm and loving nurse practitioner who took it upon herself to improve a life-threatening process in the critical care units of her beloved hospital, Delta Care System. Each week, Patty checked the crash cart in different units to make sure she replaced all expired medications and *missing* items instantly. "It is a dangerous and time-sensitive process," Patty told me. "And I need to visibly check, replenish, and replace several items on the crash cart. Crash carts are used in emergency situations, and replenishing all emergency-related items is of critical importance to us. You see, if an item expires or goes missing in an emergency, we can have life-threatening consequences."

The CEO of Delta Care Systems, Dr. Persaud, was very passionate about digitization in healthcare. He heard Patty speak passionately about the process, and he became very excited about creating a revolutionary mobile app that could become the next sensation in the United States, if not the world. So, he hired an advisor, Paul, to automate and standardize the crash cart process. Over dinner and drinks, the CEO and Paul discussed the possibilities of this incredible invention with the chairman of the board. Paul launched the process to create the LifeApp, and he invited a group of aspiring clinicians to assist him in the process. The only missing person at the table was Patty. Paul did not involve the *one* person who had the interest, experience, and knowledge to improve the process. Patty joined the process late and asked too many questions. She doubted the effectiveness of fully replacing human intelligence with the app. Paul insisted on pushing the app forward and paid little attention to Patty's objections. Twelve weeks later, the CEO and Paul presented his genius LifeApp to the leadership team.

The LifeApp was well designed, but it failed to meet its promise. It went on to win national transformation awards, yet in reality, the app created unnecessary rework for nurses and for the material management team. Nurses complained about spending too much time manually documenting in the app. It was easier to go back to the manual process. During an AHCA visit, representatives from regulatory boards identified life-threatening misses that the LifeApp had failed to catch. The emergency room was cited for lack of compliance with the crash cart process for the first time in twenty-one years. Without the end user's input, change fails.

Patty told us, "I was left out completely from the process. When I shared my concerns at the management meeting, I was pulled out of the crash cart process and my boss took over. They even received an award, and I was not invited to the ceremony. I found out about it from the company newsletter. It was heartbreaking for me. Everyone was there but me." Patty sighed. The disappointment was evident in her voice.

"So does the LifeApp have a chance?" I asked Patty.

"Absolutely! It is a great idea. They just needed to listen to the nurses who had been working on the crash carts for over fifteen years," she said as she laughed out loud.

When you ignore the end user's perspectives, you sacrifice the opportunity for transparency. Whether it is our drive for results, our passion for innovation, or our overconfidence in technology, we may trap our intentions in a closed tunnel. The passionate expert feels abandoned and disrespected when he or she is expected to accept orders with no freedom to share their perspective about the change.

Change demands energy-energy to launch it *and* an equal amount of energy to sustain it. The cycle of change evolves, matures, and claims a new life over time. Launching the change effort requires intense effort; making the change last is another. During organizational change, the area of greatest risk is when *every* project becomes a priority. Stay focused on what is a priority and make every effort to rid your bottom line of what is not. The plethora of vague goals and unclear deliverables is all too prevalent. The whole leadership team must be clear and committed to the purpose of the change effort. The main reason behind success is usually a solid alignment to one leading priority at one time. Having too many priorities is an oxymoron.

Unprecedented change brings along unprecedented possibilities. Today's competition is vicious, and client engagement is more demanding than ever. We're in *constant competition* for faster, better, more efficient processes yesterday. Change is inevitable. And the risk of a failed launch increases as we rush through change and cut corners to meet deadlines. The drive for change has brought *tremendous* attention to the cost of rushing during high-stake projects. There are better ways to lead and optimize your next change through people-centered practices and tools.

Summary

Be aware of drivers of the crash during takeoff:
1. Misalignment
2. Lack of trust
3. Incomplete communication
4. Abandonment
5. Superficial compliance
6. The purpose gap
7. Competing priorities

We must educate the managers about the new process but we don't have time.
Email will do.

Leadership Essential 1

Connect the Dots for You and Your Team

> "Happiness is when what we think, what we
> say and what we do are in harmony."
>
> ~ MAHATMA GANDHI

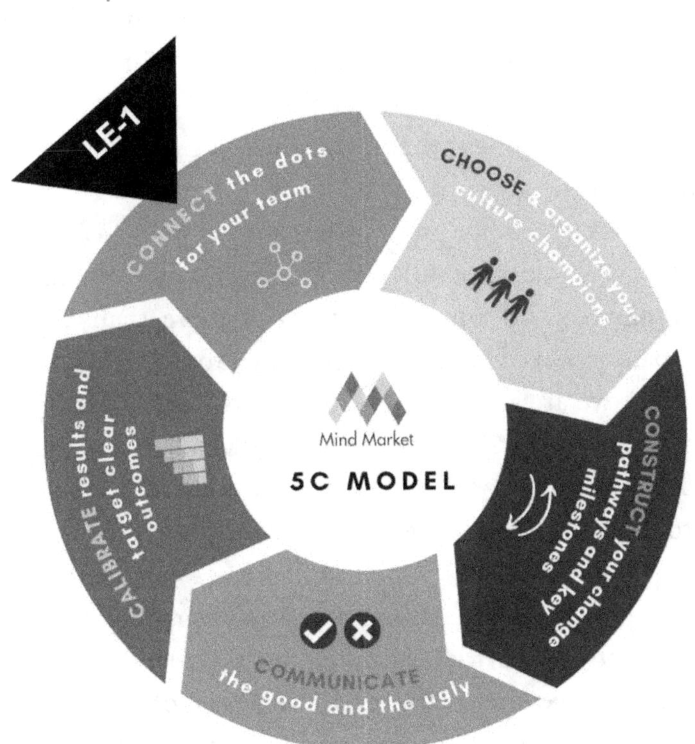

Build your vision from the Bottom Up

A study by Bitkom found that 75 percent of all IT and post-merger integration projects fail primarily due to errors in the planning phases. One reason they cite is the lack of focus on effectively *leading people* through change. Another reason is focusing on the wrong project.

Many successful companies have cracked the code of a clear vision for change. They have found a way to integrate *purpose* into their core conversations with others. They know exactly what their customers want and recognize how they make things happen for them. They realize that clarity cannot be muddled with chaos. Vision must be integrated into the DNA of the organization so uncertainty becomes an opportunity to innovate. A shared purpose is the *glue* that connects different disciplines to one common roadmap. A shared purpose is not accidental. It is intentional. These leaders invest time and resources into making change an opportunity that is larger than life, backed up with intentional cultural narratives that sing the praise of change. When you get deeply involved in understanding your employees' needs, and common blocks, you tap into the essence of inspiring change *through* them. This dialogue must happen before change takes off the ground.

Hindustan Petroleum Corporation Limited (HPCL) did exactly that. HPCL is a Fortune Global 500 company with more than 11,000 employees and annual revenues of more than $23 billion. "The company realized that we ought to change, and change drastically, so that we are able to compete with the private sector within the country," said Arun Balakrishnan, chairman and managing director. He explained, "For a long time, we were used to the customer coming to us rather than we going to the customer. Culturally, a lot needed to change."

The brilliance of HPCL executives was when they realized that the best way to get to the customer was to go *first* to their employees—to involve them *directly* in the task of overhauling the mentality that they had long operated within. At the crux of their effort was a *redesign* of top-down communication. HPCL Leaders recruited employees throughout the organization to participate in a series of vision workshops. These workshops involved considerable investment and significant risk. In their quest to empower employees to communicate a system-wide vision, they risked undermining their own authority and uncovering internal gaps and misalignment among different functions. The *determination* to promote system-wide change was not a "feel good" exercise; rather, it was intended to develop and implement a people-centered approach to change.

"Communication must reach the bottom of the pyramid," Choudhury, chairman and managing director of HPCL, said. "Otherwise, people would not know what the strategy of top management is. If we made the strategy only at the topmost level, people would not own it. And the important thing is that *everybody* has to own it…so they take it seriously."

HPCL leaders were intentional about including *every* employee. Balakrishnan shared: "That was a very earth-shaking experience. It brought the company together, with everyone working for the same cause." The results were phenomenal. The vision expanded far beyond their imagination as employees pushed for the company to go global. In essence, HPCL employees created a vision for the company that extended far beyond their original vision.

When you involve your team in creating the vision for change, you spark their creativity and commitment to the change effort. You create a cohesive team that is *determined* to advocate for change. A clear purpose can empower the masses to become drivers of change. You help them connect to a strong sense of identity. Including your teams in the creation of the vision of change is the *hallmark* of organizational transformation. The opportunity to connect the dots for your team is unprecedented. When you create the vision for change *with* your team, you *amplify* their awareness. You allow them to bring new possibilities to your plan and identify realistic blocks to progress from the onset.

> Change can no longer be viewed as a one-time inter-
> vention; rather, it is an essential and fluid management
> strategy that supports the long-term survival of your
> organization.

Inspire Their Hearts

BOBS's leaders knew without a doubt that focusing on a heartfelt purpose would create the spark they needed to transform their organization during the pandemic. Inspired by the idea of optimism and global giving, BOBS, a company that sells shoes, became an overnight sensation, when its leaders shifted their standard sales theme to a drive to help children worldwide. They sparked a charity movement that touched the hearts of people all over the world. Their message was "Using earth-friendly packaging, BOBS is designed with comfort, style, and care in mind. For every pair of BOBS shoes that you buy, Sketchers will give a new pair of shoes to a child in need." This wasn't a new idea; it was just a *great* idea put in motion at the right time. Their idea was not unique. Their marketing strategy was not new. In fact, TOMS shoes was the originator of the idea. BOBS's idea was simply timely. At a time when sales were at their lowest around the world, BOBS boosted their sales by 311 percent in 2021. A call for social impact, at a time of an unprecedented global pandemic, inspired people's hearts to be determined to support the company's initiative.

Unprecedented challenges call for unprecedented opportunities. BOB's marketing idea invited people to resonate with a *message of care.* Let go of your guilt to indulge, choose to shop with us, and we keep giving. Their strong focus on purpose, at a time of a global pandemic, was brilliant. It created a pathway to indulge and to connect through the lens of social responsibility.

"We want to contribute to a better world for everyone. We want to elevate the feeling of guilt of not doing anything," Jane, a customer representative at BOBS, said. Purpose-driven change can spark a sense of connection, a feeling of serving a bigger purpose. There is a hidden spark in *togetherness* that makes us more *determined* to change.

The roadmap for culture has become a manifesto for survival and growth. The tight labor market and unpredictable economic ups and downs add another layer of urgency. We are facing pressures of competing priorities, and work and life add a burden to people's time and commitments. A people-centered purpose creates the spark that makes your contributions meaningful. It connects you to a higher purpose. Organizations that operate with a clear sense of vision can be extremely successful.

Lead Through Intention

Livongo recognized the *power of intentions* when they created a product that became a global sensation. Livongo is an acronym for "Live Life on the Go." Livongo provides its users with a health device that immediately measures glucose levels in patients with diabetes. The client inserts glucose test strips into the device and uploads the data to the user's personal gadget to facilitate tracking, recommendations, and alerts when the user's data looks off. All this happens on the spot. Early on as a startup, its founder and healthcare entrepreneur, Glen Tullman, made health and people his daily intention, and for that, he decided to invest in some unconventional trade-offs. His purpose was personal. His son had been diagnosed with Type 1 diabetes. He made big investments for a small startup. The investment included *giving away* glucose strips to encourage Livongo's members to use the app on a daily basis. Tullman also hired a virtual care team to provide advice during emergency situations.

This purpose-driven change was revolutionary in 2014. Livongo was on a mission to help people with chronic conditions to stay healthy. For patients with diabetes, this meant regular blood-glucose monitoring to stay healthy *without* constant visits to hospitals or doctors' offices. Livongo counted on the *long-term payoff* of customer retention. Two years from launch, with excellent engagement scores from their highly committed team, and nearly $40 million in revenue, the company gained 53,000 *active* members. In 2019, Livongo was valued at $3.4 billion. Before its merger with Teladoc, Livongo was valued at $18.5 billion! This all started with a revolutionary idea to bring about *determined users* to own the change. When you elevate our purpose to serve humanity, when you are intentional about your purpose, your vision becomes a highly profitable venture.

Consider these questions as you start planning your next change. Invite your team to be part of the conversation from the onset.

> *What is my intention for change?*
>
> *What could be a higher purpose that connects the dots for others?*
>
> *Who do I need to co-create my vision with?*
>
> *Why should others follow me?*
>
> *How can I be more intentional about driving the change through others?*
>
> *How do I surround myself with people who are determined to implement the change?*

Team Identity During Change

Change has two sides. One side of change is the process side—the hardcore procedures that are essential during change. The other side of change is its people. Successful organizations rely heavily on having clear goals for the change, mobilizing adequate resources to support it, and selecting the right teams to implement it. Change, in most cases, fails not because of the process, but as a result of disconnects and confusion throughout the process.

Most often, employees make mistakes because the process is sloppy. As Michael Hammer, one of the founders of the management theory of business process reengineering, explains, "Our problems lie not in the performance of individual tasks and activities, the units of work, but in the processes, how units fit together into a whole. For decades, organizations had been beating the hell out of task problems but hadn't laid a glove on the processes."

When the tide of change becomes overwhelming, we often choose command and control over collaboration. Rather than including those who do the work to provide us with their best ideas, we start to ignore details and react to what is right in front of us. As a result, change becomes frustrating, diminishing, and a burden on frontline managers and employees.

Hundreds of business journals and blogs are filled with guides on how to ensure the lasting impact of change using one process or the other. Making change last, however, is underrated and most often overlooked. When we are faced with unprecedented challenges, our ability to lead with clarity and drive momentum, while balancing multiple demands, can be overwhelming. The common belief that processes, when implemented right, will secure a good outcome during change is limited in its thinking. The process side is one side of the equation. The other side is people.

What could predict a failed change effort? The rush to change, based on shortsighted goals and timelines, can disrupt operations. Ranjay Gulati, professor at Harvard Business School, evaluates competitive strategies of purpose-driven companies and how they *simultaneously* pursue profit. He considers the combination of purpose and process a *generative force* that improves everything about an organization. Gulati claims it may not be easy, but his research shows it works. Gulati shares the challenges Etsy, an online arts and crafts marketplace, experienced when they went public in 2015. From 2005 to 2012, Etsy had grown to provide $2 billion in sales for 1.4 million sellers each year with a top-talent workforce because of its social *purpose* and *generous* policies. Unfortunately, the company wasn't showing a profit and hadn't since 2012.

Nine months after it went public, their stock dropped by 75 percent. Their investors lost trust and patience in the leadership, which led to the appointment of Etsy's new CEO. While holding on to Etsy's purpose, Silverman, the new CEO, made the difficult decision to lay off nearly 25 percent of the workforce and shut down a number of people-driven projects. Within a few years, as gross sales grew, Etsy was able to hire again, doubling the number of underrepresented minorities on staff. Their social initiatives continued to be focused on three goals: empowering people, environmental responsibility, and diversity. Silverman shared that the trade-offs made and the *focus on purpose* and stakeholder management have allowed Etsy to become five times more productive. Gulati calls them "practical idealists" as they found a way to achieve both commercial and social objectives through purpose. At Etsy, purpose became a multiplier, informing long-term strategy, building a powerful brand, and serving as a people-centered magnet.

Change is accelerating, and managing change after change with no end in sight can be exhausting. By sharing a clear purpose for change, we demonstrate an unrelenting belief that vision is achievable, and a people-centered vision elevates your customers and employees during unsettling times. Purpose can stabilize your teams and resources by aligning their tasks to what is important to accomplish.

Change has two sides—the process side and the people side. We often overlook the latter.

As you connect the dots for your teams, three things begin to manifest:

1. A team identity around the vision. When you are engaged and committed to the change, you project excitement about the change effort and engage your teams in co-creating the pathways that translate the vision into actionable outcomes. When the team is given a "shared voice" in how the vision can be designed at the process level, the team can then articulate the vision and self-organize in a meaningful way to get the job done. *Team identity* is a powerful phenomenon that can change how your team approaches problems. Instead of a focus on the problems ahead, they can shift to solution-focused conversations.

2. Shared goals. Change requires team members to accept responsibility for making change happen in all they influence. Ownership is best created when teams collaborate and solve problems together. Ideally, when team members create their own version of the journey and identify the milestones necessary for the realization of the vision, it is far more likely for them to be determined to succeed. We often advise clients to invest time and effort in recognizing team motivators and stressors. These insights will influence the outcomes of change through the cultivation of trust, collaboration, and genuine engagement in the change effort.

3. Opportunity. We have a tendency to hold on to old habits. Our desire to resist the new is innate. Trying to embrace another change when we are overwhelmed with things to do can lead to anxiety, panic, and burnout. Mediocrity, or the absence of competing ideas, trumps opportunity. The idea of "we've always done it this way" makes sense when we are stretched. It is quite difficult to stop doing what we do really well even if it is no longer serving a purpose. Through open conversations, you identify opportunity and mitigate mediocrity.

The goal is to aim for a greater sense of employee ownership and to help the team integrate the team's perspective in how process improvement can positively impact their daily outcomes at work. Make it about them. Connect the dots for your team and *align* people toward a clear strategy. A clear strategy for the change is at the heart of alignment. During change, communication changes to tactical very quickly. We spend more time teaching staff technical skills than we spend training newly promoted managers on managing relationships and teams. The need to focus on what is needed—at every step along the way—is essential to success. Clear communication overrides ambiguity. Yet, building employee morale, managing employee resistance, and promoting trust require training and safe practice.

Team Identity

I facilitated a conversation with a global marketing team in the pharmaceutical industry. The team experienced significant changes in leadership, and an aggressive growth strategy demanded immediate intervention to re-align a global change. The team recognized that their primary resistance to change was attributed to difficult personalities on the team and a lack of trust in new team members who were perceived as not capable of managing the complex situations they faced. Understanding their unconscious bias and resistance can be a solid pathway to managing roadblocks to change early in the process. To promote alignment, we facilitated team conversations regarding team identity and resistance to change.

The process started with four fundamental elements:

1. **Team identity:** Explore the team's identity by holding open and safe conversations regarding what the team wants to stand for, what success looks like, and the payoff for team alignment and the change effort.

2. **Commitment:** Discuss what the team is willing to commit to and recognize team behaviors, positive and negative, that show up during change. Lessons from previous experiences can help the team recognize tendencies and preferences.

3. **Team resistance:** Identify resistance through team assumptions, fears, and personal biases that may get in the way of results.

4. **Team agreement:** Develop a team agreement to promote communication, collaboration, and accountability. Identify empowering as well as diminishing team behaviors.

FIGURE 3.1. CONNECTING THE DOTS FOR YOUR TEAM

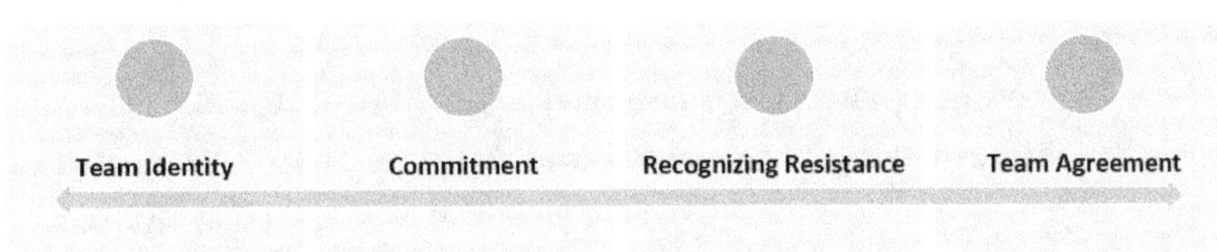

Team Identity	Draw a roadmap of desired future state: • What do we stand for as a team? • What does success look like? • How do we promote alignment and collaboration? • What's the payoff ?
Commitment	Clarify commitment to creativity, curiosity and collaboration: • What tasks can be eliminated? • What needs to be a priority? • What have we learned from past experiences?
Recognizing Resistance	What assumptions or competing priorities might get in the way? • Fear of failure • Fear of losing control • Fear of competing priorities • Lack of support/resources • Conflict among the team • Personal beliefs or past experiences
Team Agreement	What do we start doing? What do we stop doing? What do we continue doing?

Figure 3.1 provides you with questions to ask when you facilitate conversations around team identity and to develop a team agreement that recognizes resistance and the roadmap for commitment. Open dialogue mitigates resistance. By helping the team openly voice their feelings about the change, they begin to embrace collaboration. Ignoring this step or showing low tolerance for their concerns can breed resentment and mistrust.

We invited the team to share their experiences with change so they can embrace the new. We used the time reflection framework to acknowledge the diversity of experiences among the team.

1. **Make peace with the past.** Allow time for the team to share their frustrations and validate their concerns, not ignore them. In other words, make peace with the past.
2. **Claim the present.** Articulate the roadblocks the company or team faces today and how the change will remove those barriers.
3. **Honor the future.** Connect the dots for your team and create an agreement to help them design an impeccable vision for the future.

Consider how you can use the team identity process to facilitate a team discussion and help them explore ways to claim the present and honor the future. Walk them through each element of team identity so they recognize their perceptions about the outcome and align them toward a clear vision for how to operate as a more effective team during change. Figure 3.2 illustrates a live discussion I facilitated with a clinical leadership team that was about to embark upon using Artificial Intelligence to support their notetaking protocols.

Figure 3.2 shows a real-life example of a team discussion I facilitated around identity, commitment and resistance. The team agreement was based on a Start-Stop-Continue process to identify common

FIGURE 3.2 SAMPLE OF TEAM IDENTITY DISCUSSIONS

Team Identity — Commitment — Recognize Resistance — Team Agreement

Team Identity	• *We are high functioning, collaborative and resourceful.* • *We solve problems together. We are a well-oiled machine.* • *We are experts in our field. We anticipate change and support innovation in our field.*
Commitment	• *Dedicate time to solve problems.* • *Say what you do and do what you say.* • *Address challenges with an open mind.* • *Speak to each other, not to the boss.* • *Assume positive intention. Stay curious.*
Recognizing Resistance	• *I am better. I am smarter. I have more experience.* • *I avoid conflict during change.* • *I procrastinate. I give good excuses.* • *I tend to criticize. Not letting new staff grow.* • *I don't have the resources to support the change.*
Team Agreement	• *We meet once a month to solve complex problems.* • *We plan face to face connections to mitigate resistance.* • *We reach out to each other for support.* • *We listen, validate and clarify intent without criticizing.* • *We are visible to our team. We share one message.*

behaviors the team recognizes as critical to their transformation. Your goal is to invite your team to co-create a team agreement that propels them forward. When they own the change, they become *determined* to make it work. The collective contribution of the team can mitigate resistance and promote commitment to a new change. It also helps clarify priorities, preferences, motivators, and stressors during change.

FIGURE 3.3 SAMPLE OF PERSONAL COMMITMENT

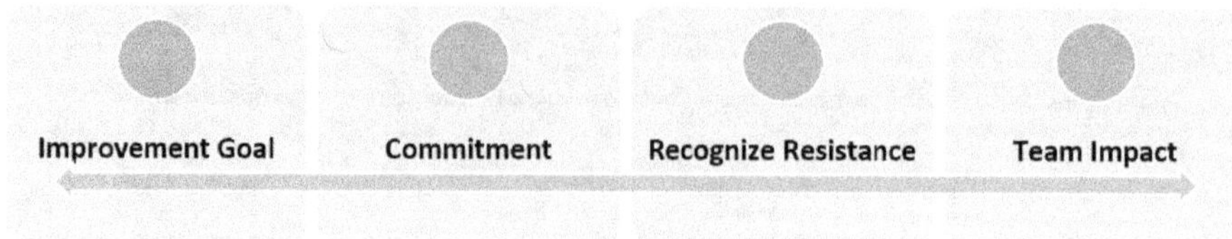

Connect the Dots – Individual Manager – Delegation Example:

Improvement Goal	I want to be better at delegating and with that skill, create opportunities for my team to grow.
Commitment	<ul><li>Clearly explain what will be delegated and why in one-on-one and group meetings.</li><li>Prioritize delegated tasks/projects based on importance and individual ability.</li><li>Follow up regularly to monitor progress and recognize achievements.</li><li>Provide training (individual & team) as necessary.</li><li>Measure the impact of delegated tasks and team growth</li></ul>
Recognizing Resistance	What assumptions or competing priorities might be getting in my way?<ul><li>I am uncomfortable with conflict when there is a difference of opinion.</li><li>It takes too long to train someone else when I can do it better and faster.</li><li>They are already too busy and will push back on added tasks.</li><li>Fear of losing control – they don't know enough to get involved.</li></ul>
Team Impact	My team will build greater competencies and become more comfortable taking on additional responsibilities. I will be more available to identify learning and promotional opportunities for myself and for my teams.

You can also use the tool to coach your manager or specific key stakeholder regarding their perceptions and beliefs about the change (See Figure 3.3). By inviting a team member or leader to reflect on the change, they can recognize their personal commitment, fears, resistance and the impact on the team.

People-Centered Conversations

Make space for your teams to acknowledge their challenges *together* before you drive the conversation toward embracing the new. When teams feel respected, they become more engaged and determined to push through obstacles and get things done. Paying attention to their experiences during change has been proven to impact how vested your team is in supporting your agenda. A shared team identity can create the right momentum for embracing another change. When you invite collaboration in designing the roadmap for change, you help them shift their thinking from *victims* of change to *drivers of* change.

I sat with Peter, VP of Marketing, to discuss his global strategy. He shared his sincere commitment to allow time for autonomy during his monthly team meetings. He felt the need to capture time to reflect on the past, honor the present, and inspire the leap into a promising merger. "I want to make it safe for my team to bring up the *messy* stuff. I want to respect that, and I want to allow them time to share their opinion openly," Peter said to me. He was not easily intimidated. In fact, he invited his executive team to share their concerns openly. That was quite a relief for the team.

His team was eager to talk about challenges, and I could sense Peter's frustration as the "messy stuff" started to unfold. He told me afterward, "I am used to working in an orderly manner. Leaving matters *unresolved* is frustrating to me. I plan for order in the meeting. I structure the agenda to avoid chaos at all cost." He shared his disappointment with the lack of closure and was concerned that the conversations got out of hand. We discussed how his strong commitment to order might create mediocrity and lack of *autonomy*. Peter's self-awareness was admirable. He was quick to recognize that his fear of uncertainty might have created mediocrity and stifled creativity during his meetings. Peter created a team agreement with his team and committed to adding 'team reflection' time to the agenda.

Sometimes, the vision for change is not clear, and we miss the opportunity to orchestrate a symphony where every player contributes to that magnificent piece. The sounds of misaligned tunes can creep into existence. Stifling your team's frustrations can lead to misalignment during change.

> Uncertainty is a pathway to clarity. Allow the messy stuff to surface and re-align your team's identity.

One Vision for Change

When you elevate your team's actions to a vision that is bigger than the change itself, you win their hearts. Win their hearts and change the world. There is an evident spark in togetherness and a hidden rift in the work of silos. BOBS's leaders knew that a strong purpose for change would create the spark they needed to transform their organization. During the pandemic, the company became a global sensation inspired by the idea of optimism and global giving.

The stress that comes with rapid organizational change can test the resilience and morale of just about any employee regardless of their job title. The jobs of 911 emergency service dispatchers became intensely stressful during the pandemic. 911 dispatchers regularly make life-or-death decisions, deal with emotional callers, and communicate consistently with the police. 911 dispatchers are considered clerical workers and may not be viewed as essential workers even though they deal with the same type of trauma as police and emergency responders. It is not surprising to know that over 40 percent of call dispatchers experience high levels of burnout.

A joint study from the Work and Well-Being Initiative led by Harvard School of Public Health and MIT Sloan explored how a sense of social belonging could reduce 911 dispatcher burnout and improve turnover in nine cities. The role of dispatchers became quite essential during the pandemic, and losing their knowledge and expertise was considered devastating to operations. To bring a sense of common purpose to the team, dispatchers received *one email* every week for six weeks from their supervisors. The dispatchers were invited to support their peers by sharing stories of challenges they faced, comments about lives they had saved, and reflections about the value of their work. They developed an online platform where dispatchers built social connections and found links to stories shared by their peers. Three months after the study, 911 dispatchers reported a significant drop in burnout, and their managers reported a 50 percent increase in retention. Supportive coworker relationships and social belonging served as a significant source of resilience and team engagement.

There is an evident spark in togetherness and a hidden rift in the work of silos.

Elevating your purpose and mastering meaningful conversations can boost team morale and drive engagement. Now imagine using this strategy to elevate the purpose of your change initiative. For example, say the organization wants to upgrade to a new virtual platform. Asking frontline employees to use a different format for chatting may have no relevance when they already use text in a familiar platform. Making your message appeal to their needs can drive momentum. Sharing the intended goal as "We want you to have less screen time and more time connecting to our patients and families" may create more engagement around the change effort. Or "We want to eliminate energy-draining emails and spend much-needed time on finding solutions that matter most to you" sounds much more effective. Your goal is not another investment in technology; your goal is to *get better results*. Telling your technical team that you are looking at a 12 percent decrease in their daily screen time so they may dedicate the time to more impactful projects may be more enticing than informing them through email that you have one *more* form for them to complete daily.

The less-is-more philosophy is relevant when creating a common vision for change. Sending unnecessary emails about the change creates frustrations, denials, and disengagement. Most people tell us they simply hit "delete" as soon as they see an email from HR come through. They stop listening. Choose to be intentional, rather than technical, about the impact of your next email. Make each message count. Win their hearts, use their words, and watch the shift happen. Focusing on what matters *to them* elevates the impact of change. Being connected to your frontline employees, understanding their pains and what makes them tick, will create a strong emotional bond so they want to commit to the change.

A capable change culture is not accidental. It is a work of art. Being intentional about your team's culture starts with creating a clear purpose that everyone on the team can clearly see, hear, feel, and articulate. We may push the bar too high to initiate urgent change, and we might start to micromanage when stakes are high. However, the spark happens with leaders who inspire, influence, and share an impeccable vision of the future. You want to connect the dots for your team so *they* implement the change. Clarity mitigates confusion, resistance, and missed opportunities during change.

> **A capable change culture is not accidental. It is a work of art.**

Constant rush and quick fixes cause undue hardships on middle and frontline employees. This fast-paced, get-it-done-now mentality calls for a pause. Take for example the Titan Submarine. Destined for world fame, the submarine instead exploded, taking away the lives of one pilot and four world-famous passengers. The pressure to move forward, the addiction to high risk, and the lure of public fame clouded the cautionary warning of risk-averse engineers. The rush to make change happen can lead to disastrous effects when we stop listening.

The constant call for managing crisis and chaos, compounded by bold expectations, is forcing managers to deal with multiple changes, last-minute shifts, and unexpected outcomes at odd hours of the day. The rush can damage relationships and compromise your influence in the workplace. So what is one thing you can do differently? Start with a pause. Resist the urge to tell them what to do, instead plan time to facilitate team identify conversations with your team. Invite them to call out roadblocks and resistance to change so you elevate your team's experience and drive their results based on reliable data generated by capable expertise within your team. Avoid unnecessary rework through open channels of communication based on mutual trust and respect. Bringing clarity to the change and connecting purpose into the latest plan iteration can help teams stay *aligned* and responsive to evolving alterations.

Involving highly diverse teams in *planning* the change can be quite rewarding. Jason Citron, founder of Discord, a platform provider for independent groups to collaborate and share, has the furthest thing from a linear story in his founding of the billion-dollar company. Discord was an iPad game that transformed into a chat platform. It all began when Jason and his team were developing their free-to-play iPad game, *Fates Forever*. The team was struggling with their existing Voiceover IP (VoIP) options. To solve this problem, Jason developed a chat service that provided a secure voice and text messaging service for his team. That triggered the start of a chat app for gamers. The much-anticipated *Fates Forever* game failed to turn a profit during launch in 2014. After much deliberation, and open dialogue about misconceptions during launch, the team decided to dismantle the software and monetize what they could. It was then that the team realized the *uniqueness* of their chatting software, and so Discord was born.

The team decided to market Discord as a free voice and text chat application for gamers to use while playing live. This was by far the *best* decision they could have made. This low-band, high-quality VoIP audio that Discord offered for gamers hurtled to the top of charts worldwide after its release in 2015. At a time of significant competition, a highly determined team was able to turn a failed attempt into a global success.

People Drive Change

Process is one side of change. The driver side is people. Change happens when the right behaviors permeate and live in the trenches. We can force change to happen, but we cannot sustain the change effort without a sincere commitment from the front line. One fundamental enabler of organizational change is the culture's readiness to embrace and sustain the change. We can empower change by making sure that the strategy is crisp enough and supported to see the change through. Driving organizational change requires a clear focus on people's readiness for change and a succinct communication strategy about the future that speaks to all stakeholders, not just those at the top.

As new priorities surface, change becomes an intrinsic part of everyday life in the organization. It becomes imperative to empower lower levels of the organization to engage in the change process. "Telling and yelling" may work for a while, but taking the time to engage our teams to believe in our vision will have a stronger hold.

The social media app that has captivated generations with unparalleled success is now known as TikTok, a political football attracting global attention. Before TikTok, there was the Chinese app Douin, which had around one hundred million users and over a billion views per day. This was the pivotal moment when ByteDance, the company that owned the app, took an interest in the international market. And so TikTok was launched in September 2017. So why didn't we hear about it until much later?

Officially released in August 2014, Musical.ly would set the foundation for the TikTok app we know today. Musical.ly started as a forum for users to record short videos where they could lip-sync to the latest popular songs and interact with one another using trending sounds and hashtags. ByteDance and Musical.ly were a match made in heaven. Spending over a billion dollars, Musical.ly merged with TikTok on August 2, 2018, and what once was a lip-singing app became an overnight sensation around the globe. Just like that, the world's number one social media platform was born.

People-centered leaders promote stronger coalitions among employees to support their strategy for transformation. When we become intentional about empowering the team, we become capable of nurturing the space for safe dialogue and for creativity to take place.

Case in Point—Connecting the Dots

Yasmin is a super-talented, smart, and well-regarded AVP in a large university system. She oversees operations, with over 400 employees reporting to her. Yasmin's day starts at 8 a.m. and ends at about 10 p.m. In between working hours, she takes care of two home-schooled children and her elderly mother. She receives more than 300 emails a day and admitted to having 1,900+ e-mails in her inbox. Her inbox has been the center of her concerns lately during our coaching sessions. More importantly, however, is one high-risk project that her team has been struggling with. The project is six months late and 18 percent over budget. "Why is that happening?" I asked Yasmin, and she responded in an anxious tone, "Well, lately my boss Alex has been way too involved in the weeds. He describes himself as a hands-off leader, but he continues to ask my team for more changes to the plan because of another great idea he has."

Alex has changed the plan four times in the last quarter. Yasmin's team is scrambling at the last minute to launch *the* most critical project they have for the year. Yasmin is ultimately responsible for this initiative, and she recognizes that every shift of focus sets her team backward.

Yasmin's frustrations are valid. Alex understands the vision but does not necessarily have the awareness of how his frequent idea-generating meetings confuse the team and derail progress. Yasmin feels accountable but not in control.

Alex is known for his brilliance and visionary thinking. In this case, his strength has become a liability for the project. Overmanaging a critical process when stakes are high can derail the effort. When changes to the original plan are introduced without regard to cost, time, resources, or strenuous rework, the results often lead to delays, and most often failure.

1. How can Yasmin connect the dots for her team?
2. How can coaching help Yasmin shift from blame to empowerment?
3. If you were Alex's advisor, what actions would you recommend?

Tools for Talking During Change

Tool 3.1—Questions Before the Launch

First, answer these questions on your own. Then, invite your team to explore these questions in an open and safe manner. Avoid interrupting your team as they try to make sense of the change. Take notes and share your perspective at the end of the discussion.

1. Why is this change necessary?
2. What problem will the change solve?
3. How do we know when the problem is solved?
4. What does this change effort involve?
5. What factors could be forgotten during the change?
6. What should we stop doing?
7. How does this change impact you and your team?

Tool 3.2—What Belongs on My "Stop Doing" List?

During your planning meeting about change, ask the team what actions or tasks can be eliminated within the scope of the project. This can, at a minimum, provide two things: solid barrier-breaking ideas, and a chance to laugh when given permission to offer outrageous suggestions. Put blame at the top of your "stop doing" agenda. Analyzing project failures may be necessary to adjust the plan; however, blame is debilitating. Discuss with your team what you want to achieve and allow them to provide their input in a safe and nonjudgmental environment. Write all their suggestions down even when you don't agree with them. Decide on your action plan based on an open team discussion and use a simple voting tool to decide on your final action plan.

Tool 3.3—What Are Possible Barriers to Change?

This team activity is about exploring the change from the personal perspective of your team members and understanding their different perspectives about the change effort. Often, we override or ignore this during implementation. One barrier that people usually don't talk about or express is the fear of losing what they control or loss of stability.

- Reactive change is often prevalent in organizations.
- "Just do it" orders lead to less team commitment and productivity.
- Inability to express concerns fully can lead to unpredicted resistance to change.
- Conflicting priorities can create frustration and resentment during change.

Explore all barriers of change and design an elevator speech the leadership team can share openly and consistently to invite people to talk about the change effort. An *elevator speech* includes the purpose of the change, the impact of the change effort, the process for implementing the change, and the timeline for the change to happen.

Tool 3.4—Handling Breakdowns

In any major project, you expect problems or breakdowns. When you openly acknowledge and communicate about breakdowns, the energy among the team shifts from blaming to solving them. Plan time on your team's *calendar* to openly discuss breakdowns. These meetings happen weekly and are intended to be short. Ask the team to identify a breakdown, explore the impact, discuss the opportunity to readjust, and resolve conflict in a caring and dignified manner. Allow each team member to benefit from the learning, not shaming or blaming, to help break down silos and maintain momentum.

Tool 3.5—Project Overwhelm

Plan a well-timed pause during meetings when you sense that you or some team members are overwhelmed. When you feel overwhelmed, it is highly likely that the team feels it as well. Before meeting with your team, pause and reflect on what is going on. Write your thoughts down so you can be clear about what is challenging to you. This way, you make better use of your time during the meeting. Be clear on what you want to accomplish and be willing to ask for help. Identify the uncertainty in your priorities and realign your team's priorities to yours. Discussing your priorities with your team will provide clarity and eliminate uncertainty. It will refocus the team on what is within their control. *Uncertainty is an emotional amplifier.* Whenever you act out of emotion, you tend to make brash decisions. Not surprisingly, when projects are rapidly changing and collaboration becomes less intentional, errors tend to increase. Regular and ongoing communication is critical.

Tool 3.6—The Decision-Maker Manager

It is natural for team members to rely on the manager for decisions because:

1. They believe the manager has all the answers, and
2. They want the manager to take control of the problem and solve it. It is a proven way for employees to get off the hook.

Avoid the tendency to become the *sole* decision-maker on your team where every member of the team is *dependent* on you to move forward. Solo decision-makers tend to keep all ideas within their hold and unintentionally seek a sense of dependency from team members. The classic *Harvard Business Review* article, "Who's Got the Monkey?," spells out the dangers of taking on what belongs to your team. When we get caught up in the weeds, we undermine the talent around us and stop natural progression. In any business process, there are hand-off zones. This is where errors and time delays occur. Making certain everyone understands what part of the process they own is vital during change. A hand-off can be a point of breakdown in the process, and identifying all hand-off points can serve as a practical exercise during team meetings.

Tool 3.7—Managing Emotions of Change

Prepare a dialogue in advance that shows two opposing perspectives about the change effort. During the meeting, two participants act out each perspective of the scripted dialogue. Invite them to add their two cents as well. Follow these steps to ensure understanding and sharing of new learning:

1. Invite the group to discuss how they perceived the interaction between the two employees and to share their

feelings about the change effort. Do not try to correct how they feel.

2. Invite the two participants to share with the group how each of them perceived the other's point of view.

3. Invite the two participants to use a more collaborative approach to discuss the change effort and to focus on a win-win approach for the conversation.

End the discussion with an exploration of ways the team can communicate using a perspective of collaboration and resilience during change. Also explore ways to mitigate frustrations and conflict among the team members.

Summary

Connect the dots for your team:

1. Build the vision with them, not for them.
2. Communicate one purpose for change.
3. Be intentional in your communication.
4. Hold team conversations about their identity, resistance, and commitment.
5. Design a team agreement that supports the change effort.
6. Lead change with intention. Be consistent about your message and actions.

Can you train them on resilience during change?
Our seasoned teams are having a tough time with the change. It's a lot to take in.

Leadership Essential 2

Empower Your Culture Champions

"Culture isn't just one aspect of the game.
It is *the* game."

~ LOUIS V. GERSTNER, JR.

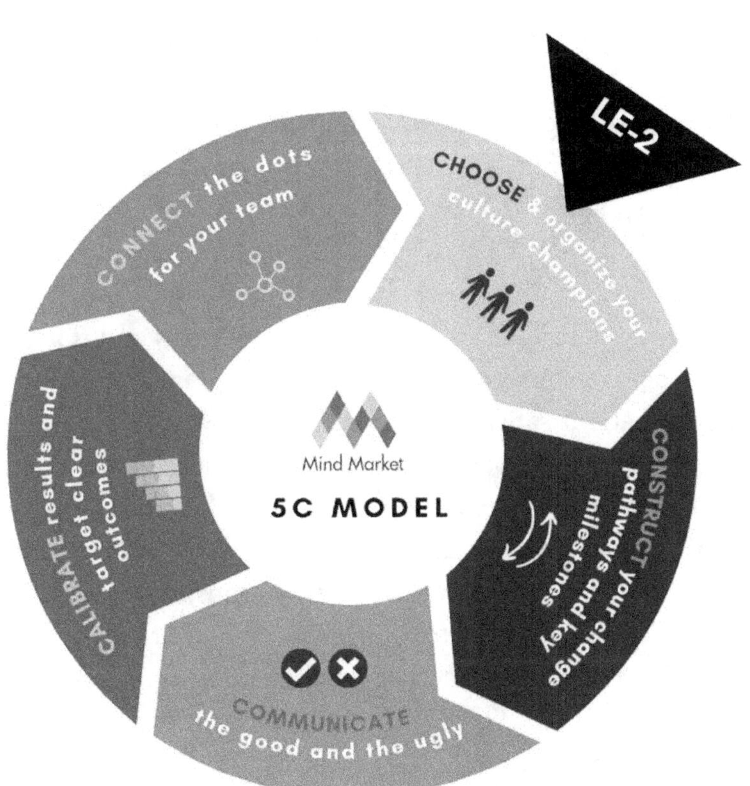

On one of my performance improvement audits through the ICU, I asked Maria, a trusted and high-performing nurse manager, how she was dealing with the frequent changes in operations. She took a long breath and said, "At least two nurses leave frustrated on any given day. There is so much going on, and we are feeling overwhelmed. Too many urgent deadlines and new policy changes. Morale is poor. The new nurses tell me this is not what they signed up for. It feels like we live in crisis mode. Add this new process, document that, train them on this new procedure. We can't keep up. My physicians are frustrated, but no one listens. When the change does not work, instead of following up, they add more change. There is no follow-up. I know you're going to encourage me to talk to my manager. I can't say this to my manager anymore because he is not listening. Dan does not like conflict. I'm the troublemaker. Dan is barely here. He is running from one meeting to another."

Maria took another deep breath and looked down the hallway in complete despair, her hands pointing to the different reminders on the wall. I could see her face slowly turning red. "I am not sure they care about us," she whispered with obvious disappointment. "They just want us to check the box."

Maria believes nothing will change. In her perception, her senior leaders spend exorbitant amounts on what is new and do not take enough time to assess the outcomes of the previous project. They want better patient satisfaction scores, but they expect the frontline teams to work faster, better, and with rigorous quality measures. Maria is overwhelmed and it was important to help her recognize the impact of her thoughts on her actions and, ultimately her experience. Through awareness of her purpose and actions, she gradually took her power back. She requested a meeting with her manager with a focus on what is a priority and how she can contribute to the change. Her self-awareness was critical, and understanding her impact on the team was a motivator for her progress.

Maria's experience is not unique. Her disconnect is not an isolated event. It echoes the experiences of many clinical and nonclinical managers who are experiencing disconnect between a highly demanding work environment, the search for meaning, and personal well-being. Caught in the middle of conflicting priorities for too long, Maria has resigned herself to silence and no longer feels relevant. She is the missed opportunity for being the champion for change.

While there is not one solution to these challenges, holding intentional conversations with her manager can influence her decision to become more determined to promote a healthy culture of change. Her resignation has a hidden cost to the organization. We cannot underestimate the power of connections at times of relentless change. The small stuff matters. Plan one-on-one conversations with each team member. A simple check-in can make a huge difference. Culture breakdowns start with a myriad of insignificant things. Taking time to hold one-on-one conversations with your team can be the spark to shift Maria's perspective from a powerless crisis manager to a determined advocate for change.

Culture Champions

A strong team is resilient in the face of adversity and chaos. The culture of the team empowers transformation through authentic and blame-free conversations, guarded by culture champions who reduce superficial compliance and drive alignment toward clear goals. Culture champions nurture commitment when stakes are high. They mitigate the impact of negative *narratives* during relentless change.

> **Culture breakdowns start with a myriad of insignificant things. Missed opportunities to listen with the intent to understand is one of them.**

In her book *Multipliers*, Liz Wiseman refers to an elite group of people who can see opportunity and growth through others.

Multipliers include formal and informal leaders who believe that the organization has smart people everywhere who can figure things out and get smarter as they go. They have trust in people during change and optimize talent by creating an inspiring environment where people can think, collaborate, spark creativity, and instill ownership and accountability in others. In other words, they are best suited to champion change, support the culture, and inspire high-potential teams to be at their best during change.

Culture champions come in different styles and represent all functions within the organization. One size does not fit all. They bring out hidden qualities in the team and amplify less obvious *voices* within the organization. Culture champions represent different levels and age groups in a variety of cultural and professional experiences. They represent seasoned and new employees and know how to maneuver challenging situations with tact. They protect the culture and feel empowered to express concerns about roadblocks or constraints standing in the way of results. Culture champions have ten unique traits:

1. They are committed to the success of the organization.
2. They are respected by their peers and the people they work with.
3. They can easily connect to others and can turn accomplices into friends.
4. They have magnetic personalities and can influence the mood in the room.
5. They are comfortable with ambiguity and not having all the answers.
6. They can connect the dots *for* others.
7. They are confident about their value and abilities.
8. They are courageous and stand up for what they believe.
9. They bring clarity to the organization and can reduce anxiety and chaos.

10. They brighten the mood of the team and speak from the heart.

A healthy culture is intentional about developing its culture champions. Selected from different roles and levels, culture champions become promoters of a people-centered culture. They focus on elevating the experiences of people during change and have a strong desire to make a greater contribution to the organization. They may not necessarily have a clear understanding of the magnitude of the change effort; however, they are committed to support the culture when constant change gets out of hand.

Selecting the right culture champions is a deliberate process. Take into consideration people's commitment and resilience under pressure. Having culture champions is an essential step. An equally critical step is to invest time and effort in developing them to become consistent advocates of change. Culture champions must be trained to communicate effectively and promote psychological safety. Their development cannot be sidelined.

Culture champions develop the skills to navigate SAFE conversations:

1. **S**hare the overarching purpose of change and its profound influence on culture and business results.
2. **A**dvocate for safe dialogue about the impact of change in both formal and informal settings.
3. **F**oster a culture of innovation and commitment to change.
4. **E**ngage effectively in ambiguous situations and challenging people.

Culture champions are promoters of change. They have a clear desire to make a bigger contribution within the organization.

Rid Your Team Culture of the Fear of Speaking Up

Culture champions can play multiple roles during change. They can bridge the gap between the expectations of top executives and honest experiences of employees during change. Fear of retaliation competes with honest reporting. When employees feel forced to take shortcuts to meet deadlines, they may experience resentment and competition. Gaps in communication lead to unrealistic assumptions, and those who resent the intensity of timelines may accuse management of concealing the truth.

I facilitated a process improvement session with twelve directors working in the research center of a large tech system in Houston. The team complained about the ridiculousness of a new process-improvement tool they were using in the center. Each manager was required to complete an observation checklist of their team—a daily thirty-three-checkpoint that required forty-five minutes from each manager. Managers felt that this specific process-improvement tool was time-consuming and ineffective in improving the client experience.

I asked Joanne, one of the participants in the room, to explain why they continued using it. Joanne, the most outspoken manager, responded, "We don't use it. We fake it." She explained that they simply checked the right boxes. She laughed and continued, "You speak up, you get the COO upset. You comply and you get a box of delicious cookies every week." I could sense the discomfort in the room, so I asked, looking at Javier, who was sitting quietly while looking at the notebook in front of him, "What makes you do what you believe to be a waste of your time?" He responded, "I was told very clearly not to complain. It was the COO's idea and you do not want to upset him." The whole group nodded in agreement.

On that day, the facilitation took a different spin. I invited the team to consider ten more options for how they could address this innocent, yet false reporting. I invited them to share the simplest to the wildest ideas they could think of. I specifically requested that they use "Yes and" and no "buts" during the conversation. The "Yes and" approach is widely known in the Improv world, and it is intended to invite people to expand on a previous point instead of negating it. "I think you have a good idea but…" restricts the flow. The list grew in potential and imagination. Through laughter, we uncovered a few actions that could lead them to feel more empowered to make the change they wanted to support.

Consider this for a moment: The mental experience of a group of managers who spend time each day, seven days a week, completing a forced checklist to avoid retaliation. Consider for a moment, the *avoidable* waste of time, energy, mood, and cost. How could fear of retaliation stand in the way of accountability and ethics in an area near you? What opportunities are you missing today in transforming your teams into raving champions of continuous improvement? How many departments keep spending time and dollars on a failed system? What processes does your team tolerate, unknowingly placing the integrity of the team on the line?

Fear of retaliation *competes* with honest reporting.

The disconnect between the expectations of top executives and the experiences of frontline managers can be drastic. In his book *Managing Transitions*, William Bridges refers to the "phenomenon of hallucination" during the implementation of change. In other words, while you might be quite engaged in the prospect of change, the narrative of what is happening can be completely distorted from the reality of those in the trenches—the people doing the work, day in and day out.

I have observed the *hallucination* phenomenon in boardrooms and management gatherings. Leaders celebrate progress and highlight results and completed milestones, while frontline staff report a totally different reality. Top leaders often may not be aware of the loss of autonomy and transparency associated with rushed deadlines and fast change (see Figure 4.1). Boardroom reports do not measure the waste of competing priorities, misalignment, rework, and red tape. While we recognize the magnitude of the change effort, we may miss the opportunity to listen to the experiences of culture champions. This disconnect can derail progress and lead to missed opportunities. Listening to and validating the experiences of frontline managers and employees is at the core of a people-centered model for change.

FIGURE 4.1. THE DISCONNECT

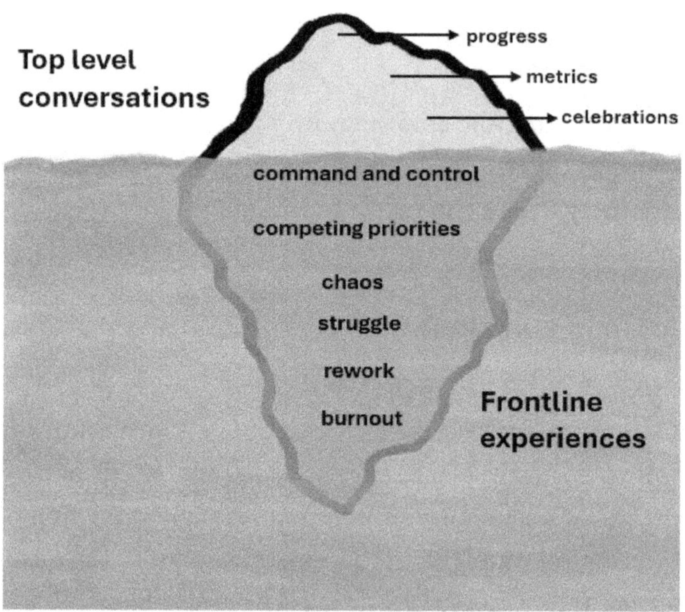

When executives celebrate the metrics and outstanding results in management meetings, they assume that their teams are playing along. In live performances, it is much easier to recognize the weak player. When leading change, finding the weak link becomes a difficult task. It requires a deeper awareness of day-to-day challenges and an intentional effort to better understand and integrate the voices of employees into the phases of change. Culture champions can advocate for change and are trained to recognize risks, communication gaps, and hidden threats. They can partner with management to fill the gaps in communication between top leadership's vision and the experiences of frontline teams during change.

People-Centered Leadership

People-centered leaders inspire their teams to commit to the change effort. They are aware of the mood on their teams and regulate their emotions based on a heightened awareness of what is *unexpressed* by their teams. They clearly understand the needs of their teams and can detect uncertainty and resistance at a glance. People-centered leaders are emotionally and socially aware. They:

1) are aware of their emotions, motivators, and triggers
2) regulate their emotions
3) recognize and regulate the emotions of others

Understanding the aspirations of others and being capable of validating them in a convincing manner, while simultaneously managing your emotions and eagerness for results, can be quite challenging. Humanity is your strategy to empower your teams to take ownership of change. Fast-moving change thrives on trust and collaboration. People-centered leaders can nurture trust among their peers and employees. Having an emotional connection to the leader can positively affect optimism and resilience during change. Emotional connections create strong social connections.

People-centered leaders invest time and effort to connect to their teams. They are empathetic and highly self-aware of their influence on others. They can intuitively perceive, understand, and use team strengths to get the results they want. They are master influencers of change. They are aware that integrity during change depends on them and others to carry the vision forward. They *trust* and rely on capable culture champions to lead, model, and show the way forward. Trust is necessary for any relationship, in any culture.

Fast-pace change calls for people-centered leaders.

Clarity Translates to Stability

Managers are challenged with engaging their teams at a time when relentless change spreads a sense of overwhelm and burnout. They are expected to promote alignment and entice their teams to focus on what is important in the projects they manage. When you manage multiple projects and enforce new policies across different functions, confusion around priorities becomes magnified. We interviewed hundreds of managers about their contributions and their frustrations regarding change. Themes were similar in many ways:

- "I don't know who to go to with this problem."
- "We need help, and no one asked us what we thought."
- "I don't want to rock the boat."
- "I didn't get training on this change. It was just 'do it.'"
- "I keep quiet and do my job."
- "My opinion doesn't matter anyways."
- "If I could speak to the CEO, I would tell him to come and observe what we do."
- "I don't want to be labeled as a troublemaker."
- "I just go with the flow. If it doesn't work, it's their fault, not mine."

Clarity nurtures stability, and stability drives focus. You may choose an empowering stance, so your team connects to what matters. Simplify your message and allow space for safe dialogue to take place. Discuss what is happening and what could be possible with your team. Recent research on psychological safety highlights the need for a communication strategy that provides information for everyone in *real time*. This is a challenge on both the process and the people side of change. People-centered leaders choose to create stability, despite chaos, for themselves and their teams. They give and receive trust.

FIGURE 4.2. THE CYCLE OF TRUST THROUGH DAILY CONVERSATIONS

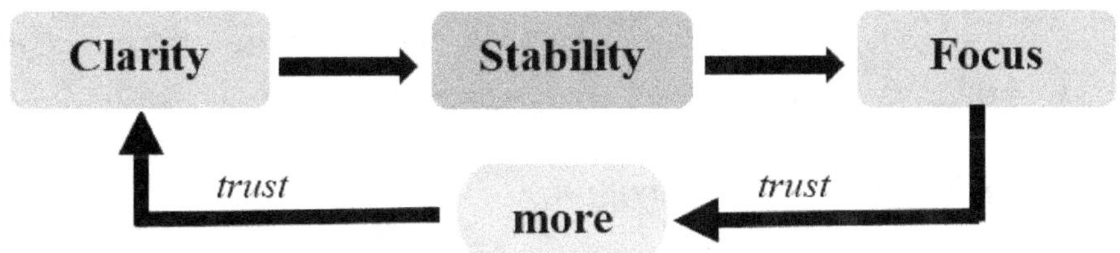

Automatic habits, by definition, are unconscious. Habits are behaviors we adopt over time that become part of who we are and our daily routine. They reside in the unconscious mind and preserve our ability to think. For example, I use the front door to leave my house. My husband chooses the back door, consistently. I asked him why he uses the back, and his answer was "I'm used to it." Complaining is another habit that we can get used to. We become really good at it over time. I have a family member who is a chronic complainer. She complains about her job, money, and her husband daily. She is well off, has a beautiful home and wonderful children, and yet she finds ways to complain about scarcity and pain. She still blames her lack of education on her dad. You probably know a complainer too. I invite you to stop and consider your habits during change. Once you have a response, ask a person that knows you well to share their perspective about your response to change.

Automatic habits, by definition, are unconscious.

We all have habits that we may not know about ourselves. Blind spots are habits we do not notice about ourselves, which everyone else knows about us. These habits are deeply engrained in our unconscious mind and very difficult for us to notice. They show up as behaviors we *seldom* recognize, unless we're very good at asking for feedback. When we feel constantly overwhelmed and stressed, and we get stuck in inaction, we may begin to form *victim* thoughts and habits. These thoughts sabotage our behaviors. They derail our trust in others during change. When we lose our sense of *control*, we lose our ability to contribute to progress. We begin to form unproductive habits that zap optimism and energy from a high-trust culture.

Five Barriers to a High Trust Culture

The first barrier to a high-trust culture is *gossip*. When you speak ill of someone who is not present, others assume you will gossip about them when they are not around. We call this the *gossip boomerang effect*. It is easy to give in to gossip because it is so seductive. It is funny at times, and it helps you relate to others who are similarly frustrated about the person in question. It also makes you feel you are part of the conversation, not left out, because of your title. It also feeds your need to know and FOMO (fear of missing out). Make no mistake, gossip is a major career *derailer*. It leads to silence when you need your team to speak up. It makes your team question your integrity and breaks their trust in your ability to lead with dignity.

The second barrier to a high-trust culture is *judging*. It is hard to listen when your intention is to respond. When we are listening to judge, to agree or disagree, or to force our point of view, we cease to listen. Not only do we do this to each other, but we also do this to the expert in the room—the one person we need to listen to. Behavior change starts with a conscious effort to let go of judgment, a choice to stay curious, and to listen to understand the message *fully*. Judgement can derail you from listening. Choosing to be present takes practice and effort. Daily practice. When you notice you are making assumptions, ask a clarifying question. *What* and *how* questions allow open-ended dialogue, which helps you understand the other person's perspective with less focus on yours.

The third barrier to a high-trust culture is *negativity*. You may know someone who is good at finding risks, what could go wrong with the process rather than what is working or what could be possible. This person has a unique talent, and their strength is absolutely needed in high-risk projects. They are not your ideal champion for change. When someone is constantly sharing their negative experience with a past project, with no ability to expand their point of view, they can zap the energy of the entire team. These "energy vampires" drain optimism, creativity, and dialogue. Beware of your language during conversations with your team. A *never good enough* mindset can also drain the potential of an entire team and create major blocks to a high-trust culture.

The fourth barrier to a high-trust culture is *obsessive complaining*. A talented complainer is pretty good about the way he or she rationalizes the complaint. It is a unique form of art. Obsessive complainers have a disastrous effect on engagement. Julian Treasure, an expert in sound and communications, refers to complaining as "viral misery." Chronic complainers drag down the team and make it difficult for people to trust the process or to rely on their natural intuitive abilities. At times, our most seasoned employees become chronic complainers when they are ignored or feel disrespected. They shed light on problems we may refuse to acknowledge or challenge us to stay curious and informed. However, the way obsessive complainers approach their team conversations can muddle the quality of the message. Listening to them can uncover valid assumptions that we may ignore due to our unconscious bias.

The fifth barrier to a high-trust culture is *excuses*. Some team members are intrinsically avoiders. They avoid responsibility, make excuses, and blame others for mistakes. It is hard to collaborate and promote cohesion with someone who does not take responsibility for his or her own actions. Their excuses sound valid—not enough time, training, or resources; someone else didn't do their part—and they become brilliant at reasoning with others. This habit normally starts at a young age, and with practice, it becomes automatic. After years of watching others pass the blame, natural excusers are unaware of the emotions behind their inaction. Fear of making mistakes or a sense of overwhelm or burnout can cause people to freeze in excuses. Managers who are good at the blame game and making excuses have a magnified, negative impact on their teams. They intensify frustration and attrition among their team members.

Our actions can help us build a high-trust culture. The more we *ask* for feedback, the more others become more *open* to receiving feedback. When we receive feedback with no attachment to being right, we empower others to do the same.

Creating a high-trust culture begins with simple acts of meaningful conversations. You can model empowering conversations, and mentor your culture champions, managers, and informal leaders to prioritize collaboration when holding conversations. The process starts with you. How you approach conversations about change serves as a model for your team. Promoting empathy toward others has a positive effect in two key areas:

1. integrating work with family and personal life
2. attention to the mental health of your employees

One of the top stressors for employees during change is the conflict inherent in balancing family needs with work pressures. Training managers and supervisors to be more supportive of the work-life challenges their employees experience can be a simple and cost-free way to improve employee well-being and workplace productivity outcomes.

Humanity Matters During Change

In a study conducted by the *joint research for action initiative* by MIT Management Sloan School and Harvard, supervisors learned new behaviors through a one-hour-a-day, self-paced, multiweek, self-monitoring exercise. They learned to listen and to express empathy about their employees' work-family demands and offered them more help to resolve challenges they faced on the job. Supervisors offered employees flexible schedules and validated employee needs during change. This training initiative had significant benefits on employee well-being and workplace *productivity*. Benefits for employees included reduced work-family conflict, improved physical health, more time with children, and improved job satisfaction and engagement. Gains were also identified for the organization. Employee commitment to change, job *productivity*, and *retention* rates increased by 39 percent on average.

What Does It Mean to Listen with Empathy?

The simple act of listening changes the quality of the conversation. It's not possible to promise someone 100 percent attention because the brain operates at a speed that far outpaces the rate of speech. There are specific habits, however, that magnify the problem, and cause you to be perceived as a poor listener. One common habit that gets in the way of listening is multitasking. Multitasking comes from a desire to be more efficient. Disciplined self-management begins with the awareness that we can be *efficient* with things but need to be *effective* with people. This is an important distinction.

> We can be *efficient* with things but need to be *effective* with people.

Four steps to help you practice listening with empathy:

1. **Be fully present.** Stop what you're doing and look directly at the person—not at your phone or gadget—when they are talking to you.

2. **Overcommunicate your listening.** Move out of your desk and choose to sit on the desk to be physically closer to the person talking to you.

3. **Validate their situation.** Express empathy through your words, tone, and body language. Convey understanding and compassion for their situation. You do not have to agree to validate.

4. **Support their journey.** Ask how you can support them. Give them the grace of space. Avoid offering advice or personal experiences; instead, meet them where they are. It is about them, not about you. Thank them for sharing and put a reminder in your calendar to check in with them at a later time.

Case in Point—Charisma During Change

Dr. Kline is a visionary physician who has an incredibly attractive energy about him. He was the new CEO of Provider Networks. He was very passionate about his vision for transformation and growth. He knew exactly where the company needed to go. Managers and employees were attracted by his charisma, humility, and commitment to creating a culture of trust and collaboration. His magnetic personality made the vision come alive across all levels of the organization.

Two years later, frontline managers started to share stories of frustration, confusion, and deflation. There were too many versions of the change effort as well as conflicting priorities, and the intensity of change began to overwhelm the frontline staff.

Dr. Kline's charismatic speeches were visionary. He was unstoppable. He was determined to get better results, yet he became quite impatient with his managers and advocates. Dr. Kline invested in his talent and had global experts on his team. "The problem is we stopped trusting Dr. Kline's intentions. I no longer felt he had my back. I think he does not care for us. It was a show. All of it was a lie," explained Olga, the business manager. "There was too much change happening at the same time. We were all fighting for the same resources. When we suffer, the culture suffers. People were retaliated against for speaking up. Each management forum became a showcase for the winner of the month. Empty promises were shadowed by fake reporting. Just fake it, the managers would say. Pretend you are okay, and you will be left alone. Just do your job," Olga shared with a quiet sigh.

Superficial compliance became deeply ingrained in the culture. Progress seemed impressive on the surface. Beneath the surface, superficial leaders were busy reporting fake results and finger-pointing. A genuine fear of being targeted for termination overwhelmed frontline managers as they saw managers they respected get terminated. Threats of losing jobs were rampant. Day-to-day execution of strategy was governed with fear, resistance, and superficial compliance. A culture of accountability turned into a culture of distrust and finger-pointing.

1. If you were Dr. Kline's coach, how would you support him in mitigating a culture of fear and fake reporting?
2. If you were Dr. Kline, how would you start to empower managers to become champions of culture?

Tools for Talking During Change

Tool 4.1—Mitigating Resistance to Change

Dedicate a two-hour meeting to discuss opportunities and challenges during the launch of a new change effort. Questions that can assist you in the process are:

1. What other changes are going on right now?
2. What could be a competing priority?
3. Who will be most impacted by the change?
4. Who will be least impacted by the change?
5. Who do we need to involve right now?
6. What projects need to go on standby?
7. How do we connect the dots for our team?
8. What do we start sharing to create buy-in for the change?
9. What problem are we not solving?
10. What are potential barriers to progress?

Invite the team to speak freely. Nurture a safe space so the messy stuff can surface, and ensure clarity regarding the vision, expectations and possible blocks to progress.

Tool 4.2—Adopt/Set Free

The Adopt/Set Free Tool was created to assist managers in understanding how change influences culture. It provides a better understanding of new behaviors that the culture needs to "adopt" and old behaviors that no longer serve the culture and would be best to let go.

Framing the change can facilitate open dialogue with your team as you explore the notion of a new change effort. Use the following questions to understand what you want to adopt and what you want to let go of. Using Post-it notes, invite the team to write behaviors they want to adopt and place it in the "Adopt" box. Also invite them to write down behaviors they want to cast away and place the Post-it notes in the outdoor section.

Discussion points:

1. What behaviors do we want to adopt that will support this change effort?
2. What behaviors do we want to cast aside so the change effort is successful?

3. What tools do we want to adopt to help us navigate the change effort?

4. What tools do we want to eliminate so the change effort is efficient?

5. How do we address conflict during change?

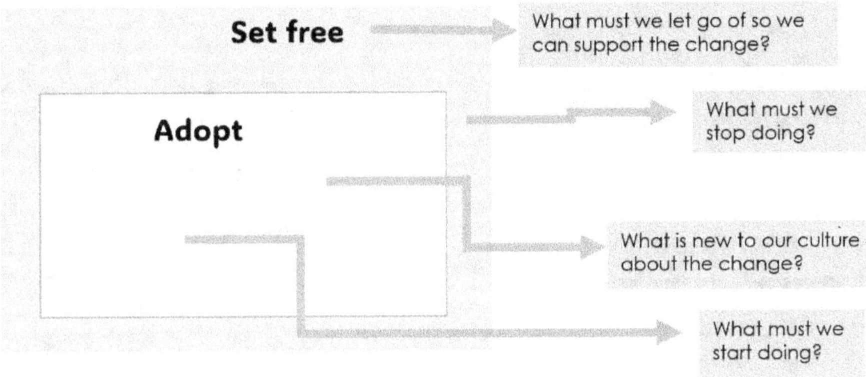

When the path is consistent, you become more prepared for the turbulence ahead. In the initial phases of change, it is necessary for us to learn to connect the dots for our teams. We do not need a glorified title to be an influencer of change. Empowering ourselves and others can strengthen the foundation to lead change through others.

Summary

Choose and organize your culture champions.

1. Develop your culture champions to drive change.
2. Drive clarity and confidence in the change process.
3. Nurture psychological safety and empathy.
4. Promote a high-trust culture.
5. Integrate *tools for talking* with your team during change.

Should we stop communicating with staff about the change?
When did we start?

Leadership Essential 3

Construct Your Change Pathways and Key Milestones

"If you want to live a happy life, tie it to a goal, not to people or things."

~ ALBERT EINSTEIN

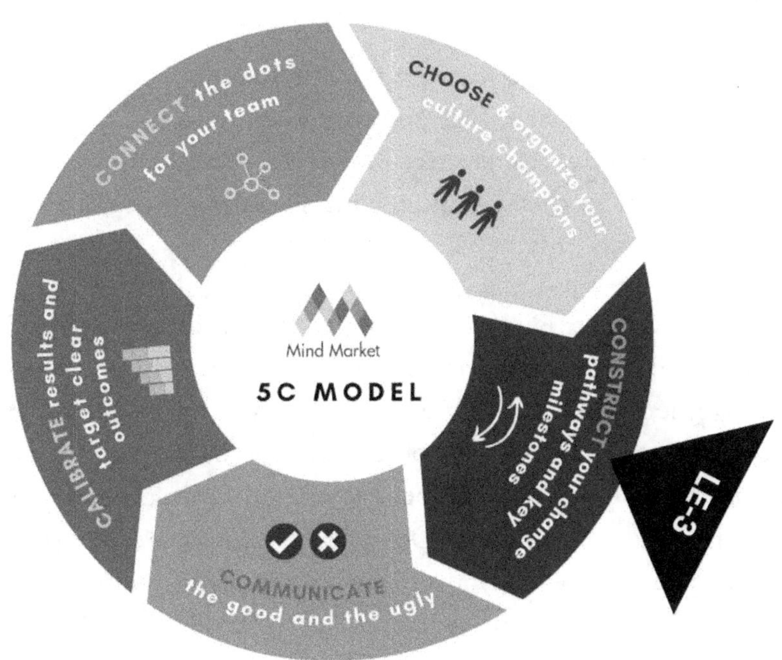

We want to take a moment to honor you and your commitment to leading change through people-centered solutions. You have stayed on course, and by now you recognize the power of being more *intentional* during the planning stages of change. You are committed to focusing on purpose-driven conversations with your team, and creating a team *identity* that allows your team to come face to face with their resistance to change. You want to honor their experiences during change. You also have, in your toolbox, people-centered tools to help you avoid the crash during takeoff. These simple yet intentional tools build a change culture where people become determined to drive it home for others.

Design Your Key Pathways and Milestones for Success

You have a destination in mind. It is usually visionary and bold and brings about a promise for a better future. Your challenge when communicating a new change is twofold:

1. Can I *clearly* articulate the roadmap for success to others in a manner that is understandable and consistent?
2. Am I *able* to co-create milestones and metrics with my team so they can fully commit their time and resources toward progress?

When the vision is clear to you and the pathways are succinct, the most important work at this point is to coach your team to work together to make your vision a reality. You map out and design critical milestones *together* so you can clearly understand the cracks you miss and align team members to operate from a place of *trust*, knowledge, and commitment. One process cannot override the other. When your team is fully aware and committed to your outcomes, they can see, hear, and influence results to facilitate a safe landing and avoid the crash during takeoff. When their expertise or opinions are stalled, issues of trust, alignment, and accountability may get in the way of results.

Make time to discuss conflicting priorities among your team and remove unnecessary obstacles for good. *Conflicting* priorities derail progress and can consume your employees with a sense of resignation. This is particularly challenging for frontline managers who may be less enthusiastic about change and are tasked with driving more change through others. Enabling your managers to share their thoughts and challenges will serve the change effort in the long run. Use these powerful coaching questions to facilitate weekly conversations with your team:

1. What is working well?
2. What is a challenge?
3. What can we remove that is no longer serving us?
4. What is a block to progress that we keep seeing, hearing, or experiencing?
5. What can we do differently?

The last question invites into the conversation the more reflective and analytical personalities in your team. While the more outspoken and action-oriented members on your team will engage and show high energy during your team meetings, paying attention to the quiet and reflective team members is of essence. These more reflective and thoughtful personalities tend to engage best when:

1. They know the questions in advance of the meeting, so they have time to reflect and think.
2. They know that you will stop and ask them for their input because you value their knowledge and expertise.

Thought-oriented personality styles (contrary to action-oriented personality styles) require more time to understand the change, embrace the new, and activate their commitment to the change. When change is forced on them through a firehose, they freeze. They either disengage, resign, or revolt. The more you know the tendencies and preferences of your team, the stronger you drive their commitment home. You begin to lead change through people strengths that overcome hidden turfs and competing priorities. You also begin to drive collaboration right into your change pathways.

Meaningful Goals Promote Collaboration

In their article "Performance Management Shouldn't Kill Collaboration," Heidi Gardner and Ivan Matviak point out that collaboration across functions and within teams is essential, to avoid the impact of ambitious silo goals. The authors recommend designing moments for the team to share best practices and ideas, so they learn from each other, and commit to work *together* to achieve collective goals. Some of your team members are ready to embrace change in a heartbeat. Others need more time to reflect, explore options, and connect with others to get the results they want.

The authors point out that in "Big Four accounting firms, revenue increased by thirty percent when collective goals were paired with changes in related processes—not the least of which was a shift from annual to monthly performance discussions, a separation between discussion of professional development and the discussion around compensation." Plan time to evaluate your goals and the competing priorities standing in the way of the results you want.

Conflicting priorities are symptoms of misalignment and hidden competition among top leaders. Tight *deadlines* do not cause the crash; lack of *alignment* does.

> Be clear about your team's preferences, tendencies, and beliefs so you tap into their highest potential.

Target small weekly goals

Empower your team to co-create clear, specific and team-driven *mini* pathways for success. Identify weekly deliverables that help the team stay focused on progress. This process overrides the sense of overwhelm that teams encounter when unexpected complications impact the whole project. Your team will focus on weekly progress and mitigate the unnecessary rework associated with complex deliverables. Rework is expected during change, yet it causes major distress when the rework effort is immense. Focusing on mini milestones allows the team to stay focused on short and specific outcomes. Uncertainty erodes trust in the team's ability to achieve results. Benefits of using small weekly goals:

- **Focused progress:** Each week, the team has a clear, achievable target, keeping them focused and motivated.
- **Early feedback:** Weekly evaluation allows for early identification of issues and course correction before significant development time is invested.
- **Adaptability:** When obstacles arise or new direction becomes available, the goals can be adjusted, and the development process adapted.
- **Team morale:** Achieving small wins each week keeps your team motivated and engaged, fostering optimism and positive conversations.

When you use small, *visible* weekly goals to tackle a big complex project, you ensure that your project progresses steadily and that your people find meaning in achieving small wins. It is a morale booster. By identifying and addressing challenges early, you begin to achieve your milestones by building more robust and effective systems.

In crafting weekly milestones together, the team maintains focus on manageable tasks that sustain the change initiative, sidestepping the overwhelming cascade of failures and fears often associated with complex and challenging goals. Stability nurtures focus, and focus drives engagement during change. That is exactly what a biopharmaceutical company did to drive human-centric change.

The world of biopharmaceutical research and development (R&D) is notorious for its complexity and long timelines. Bringing a new drug to market can take a decade or more, requiring meticulous planning, collaboration across diverse teams, and navigating frequent roadblocks. The challenge Orion Systems faced included significant delays and inefficiencies in their drug discovery pipeline. The traditional linear process, involving numerous handoffs and dependencies between different departments, created bottlenecks and hindered visibility into the overall progress.

The team used a four-step process to manage this complex goal:

1. **Visualizing the Drug Discovery Journey:** Orion Systems designed a visual board specifically for their drug discovery process. Each phase in the journey was represented by a column on the board. Individual tasks were by cards containing key information and moving through the columns as they progressed.

2. **Work-in-Progress:** To prevent bottlenecks and ensure focus, team leaders established visible status reports on the board with clear visuals of obstacles or blocks. This meant showing tasks they stopped doing and fixes that had been added.

3. **Enhancing Collaboration and Communication:** Weekly team check-ins became a central communication hub. Teams from different departments (chemistry, biology, pharmacology) held regular meetings to discuss progress, identify roadblocks, and collaboratively find solutions.

4. **Data-Driven Decision Making:** The team tracked progress using simple weekly milestones, which simplified the process and eliminated blocks instantly based on team

decisions. Color-coded solutions were used to highlight tasks to start, stop, and continue.

This simplified approach to managing a complex and critical goal can lead to a significant reduction in cycle times for each stage. The transparency of visual board discussions improved collaboration and open communication across departments, fostering a more solution-focused environment. Resource overload was another limiting challenge that the team overcame. By allowing a people-centered approach and using clear and simple weekly deliverables, the team was able to stay focused on managing resources to tackle imminent obstacles. They helped their teams visualize the purpose and roadmap for success, fostering collaboration, simplifying weekly deliverables, and limiting conflicting priorities. As a result, Orion Systems was able to accelerate innovation, and ultimately deliver life-saving treatments to patients faster.

> Taking a well-timed pause when you are overwhelmed is one of the best time management tools for reducing uncertainty—yours and everyone around you.

Cross-Functional Collaboration

At the core of internal competition and silos are annual performance measures that focus primarily on individual strengths without core competencies that emphasize teamwork, collaboration, and cross-functional outcomes. When change impacts the system, we must identify champions from different functions who can enable different teams to form and solve problems together. Cross-functional teams are essential to organizational problem solving and thinking.

Be intentional about bringing cross-functional teams together to contribute their thoughts and ideas throughout the change process.

This does not mean a free flow of ideas that derails the change effort. It means having the right controls in place to ensure that creativity is framed within the boundaries of the change strategy. Lego lost millions of dollars in reinventing itself, only to reach a 30 percent increase in profits in 2014. Its CEO contributed success to *highly engaged cross-functional* teams who approved, funded, and monitored innovation and change in a more intentional way.

Productive debate can be messy sometimes, and some of us prefer structure and timeliness to open dialogue to avoid chaos. Open dialogue helps team members shed light on subtle challenges and allows them to begin to appreciate the competing demands and necessary trade-offs to help overcome the drift. Encourage the team to learn about and appreciate different perspectives during change, before takeoff. When differences surface, most of us hold on to the idea that our opinion is the objective and correct one; and those who hold an opposing view are uninformed or biased. Challenge these unconscious assumptions and invite your team to consider these questions:

- What assumptions am I holding on to?
- What assumptions is my team holding on to?
- What is most important to me during the change journey?
- What is important to the team during the journey?
- What is important to the clients we serve?
- What problem are we not solving?
- What is one project we are working on that will take quality time from this priority?
- What tasks are we holding on to that no longer serve us?
- What insights have I uncovered as a result?
- What do we do differently as a result?

A visual representation of your findings and a face-to-face exploration of recurring themes will elevate team conversations and mitigate personal, team and operational barriers to change.

FIGURE 5.1—ASSUMPTIONS ABOUT CHANGE

	Comments	Recurring themes
My assumptions		
Team assumptions		
Preferences	Mine: Team: Clients:	
Problems we are not solving?	Mine: Team: Clients:	
Tasks that get in the way of progress	Mine: Team: Clients:	
Insights		
Action Plan		

Find time to hold conversations with your team about their experiences with change *during* implementation. Equally important is holding one-on-one conversations with reserved or quiet team members. They are more responsive in private and might offer a totally different perspective about dealing with the uncertainty of change. Invite them to reflect on their thoughts, ask questions, and offer their insights about solutions.

No matter what we do, there are times when performance feedback is necessary to address behaviors getting in the way of results. We hesitate to admit to how much we avoid difficult performance conversations or how harsh we may be in our approach. Most managers admit to learning the tricks on their own and complain about the lack of essential training on effective feedback. Managers agree that they are not willing to lose another employee, especially when recruiting a new employee takes months and their endless to-do list keeps growing. When you show up genuinely wanting to help the employee succeed, and when you intentionally create authentic connections, you become much more effective when conflicts arise.

The 4-S model (Figure 5.3), which we discuss in this section, describes how to adopt a more conversational approach to feedback. Performance conversations in a people-centered team environment promote safety, curiosity, and acceptance. They are not about proving us right, or about catching mistakes; they are about holding the space for meaningful dialogue and insights. When people are seen and validated, they are more likely to commit to change. Discussions around performance are most effective when held often and include asking for employee feedback. A one-time discussion, once a year, is unreasonable. Ninety percent of employees who trust their leaders to use feedback when driving change are more satisfied and engaged compared to employees who do not feel heard. Expressing interest in the well-being of employees requires a regular feedback loop—listening and acting on stated experiences. We hope the model can help you transform your performance conversations into engaging dialogue that leads to feeling determined to change.

The 4-S Performance Coaching Model

Step 1—State the behavior using neutral language. Stick to facts and share *specific* behavior and impact. Avoid using "you" in the conversation. This is critical and perhaps the most difficult skill to master. For example, "Marcia, I could not help but see that there has been a noticeable drop in your participation during meetings in the last two months (behavior). This appears to be impacting the progress of the infection-control project (impact)."

Step 2—Suspend judgment and solicit feedback. Ask open-ended questions (what, not why) and show a sincere interest in listening to understand. Stay curious and make sure she feels safe. Ask for her perspective (avoid wanting to be right). "Let's imagine that there are multiple factors at play here. I would love your perspective. In your opinion, what is going on? What needs to change here?"

Step 3—Seek agreement and a clear commitment. Tap into the person's intelligence—not yours—to create a meaningful solution. You may have the answer and know the best way to solve the problem. What matters in this moment, however, is how your employee (let's say Don) perceives the behavior and the solution. The solution becomes doable when he takes ownership of his actions. Listen to understand and meet him where he is to clarify his action plan. For example, "What I hear you say is you want to _____ to get back on track. Is that correct?" Pause after asking your question. Allow him time to share and confirm.

Step 4—Shape future alignment. Close the conversation with a clear agreement. Here is a process we use to help leaders be more comfortable with clarifying commitment.

1. "What I hear you say is that you will _____. Do you agree?" Wait for the person to respond. Then,
2. Shape alignment by asking: "How can I support you?"
3. Agree on a day to follow up. "Can we meet next Tuesday to check in?"
4. Thank them for being accountable and express a sincere interest in their success.

FIGURE 5.2—4S PERFORMANCE COACHING MODEL

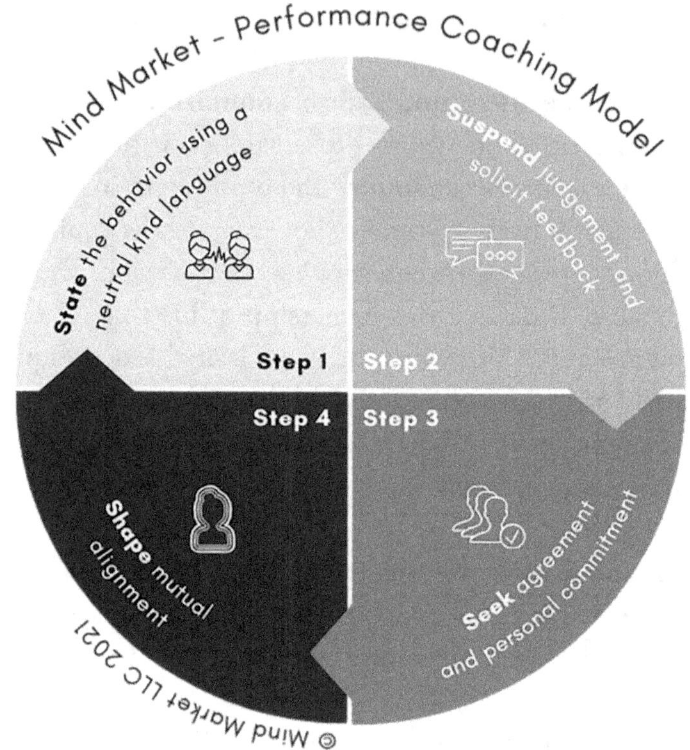

People Are the DNA of Your Change Strategy

People are the building blocks of collaboration during change. For teams to perform at their best, they must work together to implement and sustain change with a fresh sense of *shared* commitment to a higher purpose. Shared norms, shared goals, and shared responsibility will get them through each targeted milestone. Most managers we work with cringe when we talk about feedback during change. Conversations about feedback are controversial. What is important to notice is most managers believe they hold effective feedback conversations, while only 21 percent of their employees may agree that they receive meaningful feedback from their manager. We assume that what we say is being heard. Is it possible that it's not?

Feedback tends to lean heavily toward criticism, which can be discouraging and ineffective. When you are preoccupied with challenging deadlines, you may overlook opportunities to reinforce positive behaviors in the team. There's a recurring sentiment of "Why should I thank them for just doing their job?" What we know without a doubt is that what we reinforce, we promote. Appreciative feedback fosters trust, psychological safety, and team cohesion. When we focus on empowering and appreciating our teams, we win their hearts. We witness increased collaboration and commitment to change. The busier we become, the more important it is for leaders to recognize and celebrate the positive actions of their teams, as it serves as a foundation for continuous commitment.

I advised a committed new manager to start to approach feedback as information, a specific point of view that highlights the impact of their behavior on others. When you ignore the subtle behaviors that bother you in your team, you unconsciously begin to promote them. Similarly, when you ignore behaviors you would like to reinforce in your team, these behaviors begin to decline. When you focus on what they do well, in real time, you begin to influence your team to focus on what is right. You slowly diminish what is not favorable. You may have a hundred reasons to reject this concept. The power of humanity may be too simplistic to accept, and yet, we have all seen the power of humanity in action. Our humanity is in charge during change. Day-to-day decisions are made by our people. Win their hearts and watch magic happen. Focus on empowering their voice and watch the results.

Within the same context, we do not want to penalize the majority for the actions of a few. When we force all the good people in our team to attend a training on "Kindness" for the sake of the actions of the one who is unkind, we build frustration and resentment. Instead, we get better results when we focus on the person who is the culprit. The same applies to sexual harassment and diversity training programs. Many perceive the training as unjust because it is targeting the wrong crowd. Those who take ownership of their action may find the training unnecessary, repetitive, or overly focused on political correctness, leading them to dismiss its importance. Consider zooming in on the real gaps and the loud behaviors getting in the way of results. Training may be fundamental for awareness, but change happens when you hold your leaders accountable for diversity, equity, and inclusion. Your most productive manager may be the culprit, and you avoid the conversation because they hold you hostage. We do not say this is easy. It is necessary.

Can performance reviews get in the way of change?

The basic structure of any performance measurement system is designed to reflect the operating assumptions of the organization it supports. Standard performance measures may need to change to meet new culture needs. When organizations grow or change due to mergers, acquisitions, or restructuring, the need for a people-centered approach becomes imminent. Most performance systems are designed to measure individual team member performance rather than a deliberate focus on teamwork and group outcomes. We segregate individual performance at the end of the year yet expect collaboration all year long. This is what we hear from managers about their experiences with performance reviews. It is a lost opportunity when you are leading a system-wide priority. We cannot measure individual results when collective collaboration is critical to your success.

Notice what your performance reviews measure; notice what can be counterproductive to your results. On one hand you tell them to collaborate, and on the other hand you assess their success on personal outcomes. This type of performance metrics encourages competition, information hoarding, and siloed thinking among high-potential teams. When teams compete, they weaken the high-trust culture you want to promote for change to happen. Metrics that keep changing and compete against a culture of collaboration may place your change initiative at risk.

> We reward individual effort and expect collaboration all year long.

Why Do Metrics Keep Changing?

The Confidence Gap

There is a dramatic gap between what leaders think and what employees perceive to be true. Only 12 percent of CEOs are confident that their remote employees are productive (Figure 5.3). The same study reports that 87 percent of hybrid workers believe they are productive and share the burden of the pressure to prove they're working. One question for you is how to end the *productivity paranoia* and replace it with alignment at a time when our environment experiences disruptive change.

Worrying about productivity is valid. Constant paranoia about what your employees are doing is a waste of time. Some experts mock the dilemma and refer to it as "productivity theater." The Work Trend Index reports that the number of meetings per week has increased by 153 percent, with overlapping meetings to ensure employees are working. This increase in meetings is the enemy of productivity. Meetings have increased by 46 percent *per person* in the past year, and one-third of all Americans spend more than *twelve hours* in meetings each week. Middle managers spend more than 50 percent of their days in meetings *talking* about work, rather than *doing* work. They report working after dinner to catch up on *actual* work. Assess the confidence gap in your organization and facilitate conversations to reduce the gap.

All these factors can impact how organizations design and develop their metrics and indicators for success. Metrics fluctuate based on what is a top priority. Employees and employers remain split when evaluating remote work. Many leaders who miss the office environment of 2019 struggle to understand how broadly employees have embraced the benefits of flexible work. A Microsoft Work Trend Index Special Report titled "Hybrid Work Is Just Work. Are We Doing It Wrong?" talks about "productivity paranoia." Satya Nadella, chairman and CEO of Microsoft, says, "Thriving employees are what gives organizations a competitive advantage in today's dynamic economic environment. And, creating a culture and employee experience to meet the needs of today's digitally connected, distributed workforce requires a new approach." The approach includes flexible work environments that plan for serendipity to happen when necessary. A blend of both worlds can attract the talent you need from a global and national perspective, and the metrics must take into consideration your talent needs.

FIGURE 5.3 THE PRODUCTIVITY PARANOIA

Productivity with hybrid work

87% of employees report they are productive at work

12% of leaders say they have full confidence their team is productive

Survey respondents were asked, "On a typical day, how much do you agree or disagree with the following? 1 feel productive when I work' Survey respondents in a leadership role were asked, 'How much of a challenge is the following when thinking about new changes brought about by the shift to hybrid work? 'Having confidence that my employees are being productive'"

In Gallup's latest survey of remote workers in the United States, remote-capable employees expect and prefer hybrid arrangements. Along with the benefits of flexibility, employees report feeling pressured to show up more to unproductive meetings. The burden of uneven policies or inconsistent administration of policies creates a difficult and toxic environment. Brianna Doe, the co-founder of Verbatim, a global marketing company, describes her struggle with being a hybrid worker in her former job. Doe says that when she took a sick day, her manager would comment, "Well, the perk is that you get to stay home, and you still have to work." Doe added, "I had to send in exactly what I did all day at the end of the day. I had to compile the list. I felt like I wasn't trusted; it was really demoralizing." Remote workers with low-confidence managers are suffering the consequences of personal biases.

A people-centered approach calls for collaboration to transform traditional performance metrics into collaborative measures for success. The shift is necessary. The burden of change leaves employees, especially middle managers, overloaded with increasing demands. Managers do not have the authority to change the old-fashioned system, they do not have clear incentives to measure performance, and yet they are expected to engage, retain, and keep their employees fully productive. Recent research confirms that the *effectiveness* of your team performance is directly linked to the extent to which your team members have a *voice* in the design and development of the metrics.

The *effectiveness* of your team performance measures is directly linked to the extent to which your team has a *voice* in the design and development of the metrics.

Feedback During Change

I recently spoke to Hannah, a high-potential manager in the tech industry. She is very passionate about her client-facing role, and her passion for value-based client engagement is quite refreshing. Her purpose at work is clear, and she has a way of keeping it at the center of everything she does. She is now navigating the complexity of another role—managing the expectations of a new senior leadership team. Hannah reports to Mark, VP of Operations, and to Syed, the CFO. Neither of them is comfortable about holding difficult conversations that might lead to conflict.

Hannah is the head of event planning and fundraising. Her role provided her with a clear level of authority in making final decisions about her client's calendar of events. Before going on vacation, she notified her manager about an upcoming client event that was not approved. She informed the client of the decision to reschedule the event, and her client accepted the outcome. When Hannah returned from her vacation, she learned that Mark had reversed her decision. He approved of the event without contacting her. Hannah felt disrespected. She was struggling between remaining silent and accepting the last-minute change her manager had made. She did not feel comfortable holding the discussion with Mark and Syed. This type of situation is an ongoing struggle for her and her team.

I invited Hannah and Mark to meet and identify a common purpose for change and a team agreement to specify their needs for collaboration. What Hannah wanted was to feel respected and included in decision-making. What Mark wanted was faster results. I helped them connect the dots and clarify how they approached the same challenge differently. Mark emphasized the importance of the role that Hannah plays on his team and committed to listening and validating her concerns in a more deliberate manner. Hannah also promised to be more open to different point of views and to make it clear when she feels disrespected. This open dialogue allowed Hannah to define her level of authority and acknowledge her challenge with trust. The clarity helped her become more determined to own the change. They agreed to meeting weekly to stay aligned and focused on moving forward. Mark's communication with her improved drastically; so did the trust.

Being receptive to change means promoting a culture where varying opinions are expected, not stifled. When we allow our teams the gift of sharing with no judgment, we create a culture in which managers feel empowered to contribute to the change effort. They feel psychologically safe to bring up the messy stuff. Facts alone do not resolve conflict. Validating their emotions does. When we avoid holding conversations to address the difficult issues, it can weigh heavily on our teams, and more importantly, on us.

When we are excited about the change, we may not have the patience to pause and accept different points of view. Silence among your team is a choice. It does not always mean they approve. It may signal the absence of psychological safety. In other words, psychological safety may have a *direct* link to the extent to which team members take turns speaking in your meeting.

Is it even possible to embrace silence and notice the unexpressed when you are inundated with deadlines and the rush to deliver?

Considering the chronic stress many of us are experiencing during constant change, employees are more likely to focus on the sense of overwhelm in our message. Even a neutral request, "I need you to expand on that report," might be interpreted negatively and translated as, "Your work is not good enough," or "Do it the way I want."

We invite you to take a closer look into the impact of your interactions with others. How might others perceive your listening? What comments might be considered careless unintentionally? Reflect on your most recent meeting with your team. Consider these questions: "What percent of my dialogue is me listening to my inner monologue?" and "What percent of the conversation am I talking versus them talking?"

The measure of effective team performance is directly linked to the extent to which team members take turns speaking.

Leadership Pitfalls

Some leadership pitfalls are more common than others during change. For some of you, the list may be like "the story of my life." For others, the list may seem unreasonable. We suggest you ask your team to prioritize which pitfall to focus on.

1. Reactive Communication

Communicating in a strategic manner is hard—given the impact of conflicting priorities on the masses. It is easy to put communication on the sideline as we get bogged down with challenges. Once in motion, a project takes on a life of its own and naturally evolves. When managers connect the dots, they become more aligned to the big picture. Conversely, when we work from a place of misguided complexity, a feeling of overwhelm undermines their ability to take a step back to review the "big picture." Reactive communication is ineffective. It tends to be one-sided and is usually triggered by assumptions and judgment. When we become overly stressed during change, we make decisions based on what we see in front of us, with little attention to the impact of our decision on others. Middle managers can become quite frustrated when they chase after reactive decisions. When it does not make sense, when the whole picture is not so clear, they tend to feel disconnected, and experience an alarming sense of disappointment, resignation, or anxiety.

Recommendation:

Build a communication strategy *with* your managers/teams, not *for* your managers/teams. Take time to discuss goals, changes, and strategies with your team on a weekly basis so essential milestones are met. Listen with curiosity and rephrase to demonstrate your intent to understand. Nance Guilmartin, Emmy award-winning journalist and author of *The Power of Pause*, describes rephrasing as: "the art of offering someone a gift of your time and attention." In other words, help them hear what *you think* they meant by what *you think* you heard them say. Show them that you care about the meaning behind their words, and that you are not making assumptions. Listening fully, quieting the inner chatter, is an act of compassion, which can promote trust and alignment during change.

2. Judgment and Tendencies

Managing the people side of change means recognizing the capabilities and behavioral tendencies of team members. Those who are assertive and bring up the messy stuff are often labeled as troublemakers. Those who are not inclined to speak up may be perceived as submissive or disconnected. Oftentimes, both the loud and silent may add value and uncover beneficial when you adopt a more curious approach.

Recommendation:

Allow time for open dialogue. Listen to those who have different views from you with curiosity, not judgment. Your louder employee may speak for those who opt for silence. Be willing to validate team members who choose to speak up and find time to privately connect and collect feedback from those who are habitually quiet. Allow reflective individuals the space to think. Asking for their opinion privately may be effective. The ones who choose to be silent are potentially speaking in their head. Don't underestimate the power of silent resistance.

3. Manager Willingness and Capability

Without a sense of purpose, the middle manager becomes the "abandoned leader." Recent studies of upper management show that while they feel they can live their purpose at work, they are unaware or in denial about how connected middle managers and frontline workers feel about the organization or the change. Author and Nobel Prize Laureate Toni Morrison often told her leadership students, "If you have some power, then your job is to empower somebody else."

Torn between expectations from C-suite executives and the competing priorities around how to deliver specific results and motivate teams that are in panic mode about their future, the middle manager often operates without the proper tools to manage competing expectations. Learning to say no is difficult. They think that if they say, "I don't know," it could be detrimental to their career. Because of these reasons, many middle managers resort to superficial compliance.

If you have some power, then your job is to empower somebody else.

Recommendation:

Invest in developing your managers so they let go of old practices and adopt new and innovative ways of doing things. Offer just-in-time learning opportunities for your managers; invest in their coaching and mentoring so they become better equipped to influence and manage a culture of change. Align their operational and behavioral competencies to business and operational outcomes. Telling them to do something without listening to their ideas can close the door to development. Encourage them to take advantage of learning and development programs. Seventy-six percent of new managers say they would stay at their company if they were given more growth opportunities.

Tools for Talking During Change

Tool 5.1—Ask Why Five Times

Asking why five times is a method used for getting to the heart of a problem. It is a simple and effective way to determine the root cause of a problem. First, make sure the right people are invited to the meeting—the people who are *directly* involved in the work, not their managers. Ask *why* a problem occurred, and when you note down the cause, ask why again, *four more times.* This technique allows for a focused discussion starting with the problem statement (the what), followed by an evaluation of why that problem exists (the how it happened). With each why, we arrive at the causal factors.

Step 1: Start with the broadest statement about the problem. Make the statement as simple as possible. For example, "We want to explore why three employees left the department last week."

Step 2: Ask why again to identify the causal factors illustrating how it happened. For example: "Why did Laura think she could not negotiate with her manager?"

Steps 3 to 5: Narrow the questions by asking why again until you can zero in on a solution. By repeating the question, it gets to the heart of the problem.

When you share with your team your genuine interest in listening to their feedback, you open the door to a sincere exploration of the problem. Listen to their concerns with the intent to understand. Demonstrate confidence in their ability to solve problems. Be genuine and invite your team to clearly articulate how they can support the change and what concerns might get in the way of results.

Tool 5.2—Handling a Difficult Conversation

The simplest yet very difficult action you can take to control a perceived conflict is to *pause* and refrain from *reacting*. You cannot influence anyone else's behavior unless you are aware of your own. Reactive communication damages relationships. When you feel triggered, remove yourself from the situation. If you wrote a reactive email in response to someone or a situation, save the email. Do not reply. Review what you wrote the next day and decide whether your email is appropriate to send. Take time to step away from the challenge and be *very* clear on what you want from the situation. Use this five-step process to handle a difficult conversation:

1. **Clarify your intent.** Be very clear about the outcome you want.

2. **Write it down.** Write down what you want to say and how. If possible, rehearse it with a trusted colleague or coach.

3. **Pay attention to your tone.** Notice your body language and your non-physical cues. Remind yourself of what you want to achieve.

4. **Know your triggers.** Be aware of how you might react, so you remain in control of your emotions throughout the conversation. Be willing and ready to focus on the outcome.

5. **Visualize success.** Imagine how both of you would feel after the conversation.

Tool 5.3—Daily Coaching Conversations

Asking open-ended questions is one way to solicit feedback, identify the mental or behavioral blocks the person experiences, and understand the gap with no judgment. This requires a sincere effort to first understand and then validate what the person is saying. Once you have a clear understanding of the source of the challenge, you shift from asking questions to seeking commitment. You want to tap into their intelligence, not yours. It is about them, not you. What matters here is saving the person's integrity during the process. Show understanding for what is standing in their way and show a sincere respect for their opinion, no matter how different it is from yours.

Sample of Daily Coaching Conversations

1. I'm curious, what do you think happened?
2. In your opinion, what went well?
3. What could be better?
4. What would you do differently?

5. What options do you have to help you resolve this challenge?
6. What would happen if you included another team member?
7. If this is your friend, what would you recommend?

Accountability

8. What will you do differently?
9. How will you know it worked out?
10. How can I support you?

Summary

Design your change pathways and performance metrics with care
1. Avoid penalizing the masses for the actions of a few
2. Assess the confidence gap in your organization
3. Co-create your change pathways with your teams
4. Develop weekly milestones for long-term results
5. Promote cross-functional collaboration
6. Use the 4-S performance model

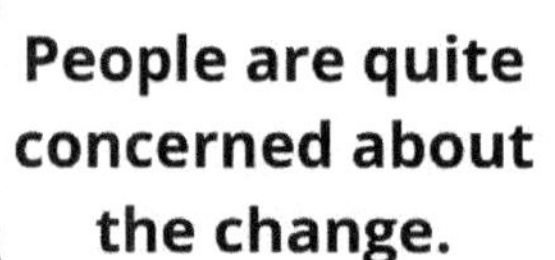

People are quite concerned about the change.

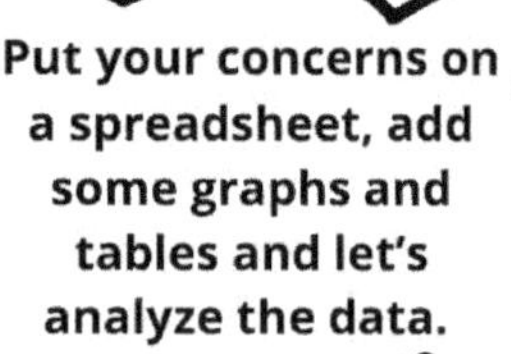

Put your concerns on a spreadsheet, add some graphs and tables and let's analyze the data.

Leadership Essential 4

Communicate the Good, the Bad and the Ugly

> "Talent is like electricity. We don't understand electricity. We use it."
>
> ~ MAYA ANGELOU

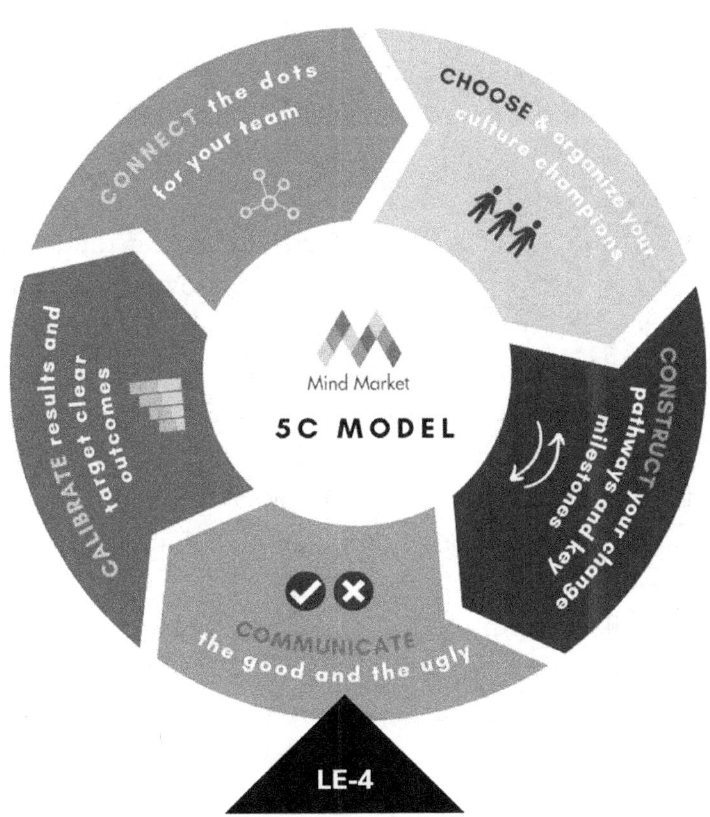

Layoffs can negate years of work on culture. The situation creates significant challenges for leadership as well as employees and their families. While layoffs are often necessary for an organization's survival, how we make decisions, and how we communicate our change strategy, sends a strong message to those who are laid off or furloughed as well as to those who decide to stay behind. Panera, an American chain store of bakery-café fast-serve restaurants with over 2,000 locations, experienced close to a 50 percent drop in revenue within one week of the pandemic. Chief Executive Niren Chaudhary demonstrated his long-held commitment to values and showed compassion and empathy as he communicated the need for layoffs. Panera "walked their talk," even in the worst of times.

Chaudhary took two dramatic steps. First, he recognized there were other employers like CVS and Walmart and more who were looking to hire. The Panera team called them and said, "We are about to lay off people who are talented; would you be willing to give them a chance to apply for temporary jobs?" The second step to soften the blow was offering employees food. For a period of time, laid-off employees were told they could come in with their family once or twice a week and eat at a Panera for free. During the pandemic, Panera reduced its workforce significantly. However, *humanity* in how its leaders managed the process continued to define the brand. Panera served 50,000 meals to doctors and nurses in New York and to half a million families through a partnership with the food bank Feeding America. One year later, Panera was able to rehire most of their furloughed employees. The founder of Panera, Ron Shaich, shared that their success comes down to three things:

1. Tell the truth.
2. Know what matters.
3. Get the job done.

You can promote a culture of *transparency* and cast a positive shadow of influence no matter how difficult the circumstance. One way is to create *meaningful* conversations with employees and strengthen their commitment to organizational change. You cannot single-handedly lead, manage, and implement change. It requires a strong *partnership* with managers, informal leaders, and culture champions to make it happen. Take the time to develop your message about the purpose for change, and start to communicate intentional stories that employees can relate to. You want to nurture relationships that help you show up as credible, trustworthy, and committed to a culture of safety. By modeling a *curious* mindset, you begin to encourage your leadership team to integrate the new into their day-to-day operations.

Gatekeepers During Change

Research on middle managers is scarce. They are the hidden talent who can elevate the outcomes of workplace change. Their development is usually an afterthought. In multifaceted work environments, the role of the middle manager in change takes on a new life. They are required to take on an added role and navigate different levels and teams to keep the change effort under control.

Middle managers are morale gatekeepers, confidence builders, and strategy translators. They play a vital role in promoting organizational change and make sure the team gets the results you want. They influence how change is received in their areas and how it will be sustained. They impact employee readiness for the change and are expected to mitigate employee resistance to it. They are the silent heroes who deal with the day-to-day complexities of the change process and often struggle to navigate the social dilemmas of managing up and down. Mark Fields, former president of Ford America, refers to them as "the frozen middle."

In our interviews with middle managers, their need to be validated and heard was profound. When they do not feel heard, they begin to *check out* from work. These mental checkouts can be subtle, yet they impact morale, reinforce limiting beliefs, and question the integrity of executives and the organization. Comments from disgruntled managers may sound like:

> "I don't care, I only do my job and get out."
>
> "They don't care for me, why should I (care about them)?"
>
> "When was the last time you saw a top leader visit this area?"
>
> "The extra mile doesn't pay the bill."
>
> "They have no idea what we do. They only care about the numbers."
>
> "He doesn't listen to my suggestions, why should I listen to his?"
>
> "I'm working on my exit plan. I shut down three months ago."
>
> "I lost two team members; I am losing more, and they don't care."
>
> "To make more money, I must leave and later come back."

Negative thoughts, over time, lead to negative perceptions within and outside the organization. People's reaction to everyday stories can become quite contagious and stifle the team, causing a disconnect between what is true and what is simply "fake news." Planning for these gaps in communication and substituting them with positive affirmations about the change is important. How you show up and communicate will lead to a renewed sense of commitment and energy among employees. Start by identifying team challenges and limiting beliefs. Notice how you react to challenges at work and replace limiting thoughts with more *empowering* thoughts. Notice what you practice daily and choose to practice empowering thoughts. Empowering thoughts can help activate solution-centered conversations.

Limiting thoughts

- "I don't know who to go to with this problem."
- "We need help, and the VPs never ask us what we think."
- "I don't want to rock the boat."
- "We didn't get any training. As usual, it was just 'do it.'"
- "I keep quiet and do my job."

- "My opinion doesn't matter anyways."

- "If I could speak to the CEO, I would tell him to come and observe what we do."
- "I don't want to be labeled as a troublemaker."
- "I just go with the flow. If it doesn't work, it's their fault, not mine."

Empowering thoughts

- "I wonder if I should ask John to help me solve this problem."
- "I wonder how I can contribute to solving this problem."
- "I want to be part of the solution."
- "I wonder how we can help them understand our needs."
- "I wonder what I need to change in the conversation to get his attention."
- "I need to find the courage to speak up and share what I think."
- "We have a responsibility to share our challenges."

- "I want to actively engage in finding solutions to our roadblocks."
- "I am part of the team. I am accountable for results."

What Do You Practice?

Sharon Babineau, my dear friend and retired soldier, is a mindfulness expert and author of *The Girl Who Gave Her Wish Away*. She shared her impeccable journey from grief as we sat down and watched the beautiful sunset in Miami Beach. Sharon experienced significant loss in her young life. She lost her husband to ALS and her sweet, loving, beautiful sixteen-year-old daughter to cancer. The journey was agonizing; it broke her free and joyful spirit.

Sharon decided to seek the wisdom of a notable monk in India. It was a long, enduring journey, and Sharon was feeling exhausted when she finally reached the monk's monastery. Sharon's heart was pounding out of control. "I had so many questions to ask, but the moment I entered the tent, I forgot all my questions. My mind turned blank." The patient monk gazed into her eyes, an abyss of stories untold.

In that prolonged silence, a profound dialogue unfolded, and Sharon heard herself asking with tears rolling down her eyes, "Why am I angry all the time?" With a gentle gaze, the wise monk touched her hand with profound kindness and whispered, "It's because you practice it, my dear." Sharon's heart sank, her frustration bubbling over into tears. "I've walked for three days," she pleaded, her voice cracking. "Please tell me something more." The wise monk, undeterred by her anguish, continued to hold her hand with unwavering compassion. In a voice barely louder than a whisper, he imparted, "Practice something different."

Sharon left the tent feeling a huge sense of relief and a genuine desire to practice joy. She did not want to live in anger. And for the first time on her journey, she saw the awe-inspiring beauty that had been waiting patiently for her to notice.

What do you practice that is no longer serving you?

Fifty-eight percent of Millennials and Gen Zs report higher-than-average overwhelm and burnout. The trend is compelling the American Psychology Association to pronounce a mental pandemic. What we practice impacts our resilience during change. Urgency falters our stability with a false sense of overwhelm. After receiving a call from his boss at 10:30 p.m., Rami, a middle manager and long-term employee, asked himself, "Is there any time during the day or night I can call him?" Rami's days were filled with urgent deadlines that left him feeling overwhelmed and discouraged. Town hall meetings painted an unrealistic picture of a highly engaged and collaborative culture, but Rami's day-to-day experience did not match what was being celebrated. "It feels like they live (pointing up) in la la land," he said.

Over time, Rami began to feel disconnected. One-on-one conversations with his boss often got canceled. He became resentful and disappointed. Like many of his peers, he was struggling with the added responsibilities. Downsizing impacted everyone and he was really scared about losing talented people. Rami began to re-evaluate his career and look for job opportunities elsewhere. He felt he was putting out fires all day long and he was no longer making a meaningful contribution. He missed the days when he was happy and believed that upper management cared.

Once trust is lost, it is not easy to regain. Rami's experience is a composite of many middle managers who are headed for burnout. It reflects on the gap between what top executives perceive and what middle managers experience within their environment. We coached the leaders to use people-centered strategies that promote trust and open dialogue. They committed weekly check-ins with their managers during the next phase of change.

The flow of positive communication has a domino effect on your teams. Factors that seem so small have a profound impact on the organization.

Working in a highly demanding work environment, with rushed deadlines and overlapping milestones, leaves no room for a pause. It causes grave errors to happen. PepsiCo had to make a public apology for its ad campaign showing model Kendall Jenner heading a group of protesters in a manner mirroring the Black Lives Matter movement. PepsiCo suffered a massive social media backlash when Martin Luther King's daughter was insulted by the lack of sensitivity displayed in the ad campaign. Pepsi experienced a significant drop in brand value. This negative story required an immediate call to action. Pepsi put a stop to the commercial immediately and publicly apologized for the mishap, referring to it as clearly missing the mark. They missed the opportunity to pilot their message with the right crowd prior to launch. The results of rushed deadlines are rampant on media channels. A time to pause and to re-evaluate and invite people with diverse points of view to express their perspectives can save companies rework and unnecessary costs.

Shadow of the Leader

Hoadley and Lamos (2012) developed an information flow model that was intended to support successful change. The authors suggested that when information flows among all internal and external stakeholders, and when clear information guides a strong coalition for change, it empowers all individuals involved in the change effort to better understand the need for change and to commit to it. The information of communication flow related to three areas of change:

1. The vision for change
2. The contributors to change
3. The operational systems supporting the change

Risk begins when one of these ingredients is missing. Michael Ming, the COO of a local insurance company, experienced the impact of a failed change effort when 65 percent of his senior leadership team was terminated. He asked me for my opinion about the reason behind the failure, and I asked him for the strategy for change and the aspects of communication used *prior* to takeoff. Michael became quickly agitated with my questions. Michael questioned my reasoning: "We did not hire you to point out the problem as our leadership team; we need tangible reasons for the resistance of lower levels to change." He shared example after example of where he thought the real problems resided. He blamed the issue on middle managers who were neither accountable nor capable of managing their influence within their teams. He was frustrated with their lack of courage, and their fear of conflict. He was quite disappointed with the financial strains they caused.

I took a piece of paper and quietly sketched the concept of the shadow of the leader. Culture is the work of leaders. Leaders transmit their conscious and unconscious thoughts and behaviors to their managers. Managers reinforce what their leaders model and reinforce. The shadow of the leader drives the values of the culture. Leadership values and beliefs cascade through the walls of the organization and become the point of reference for what behaviors we tolerate or reinforce within our teams and with our clients. When senior leaders model respect and integrity, it is cascaded to different levels of the organization. And when leaders model lack of integrity, shortcuts are mirrored across all levels of the organization. The leader's shadow is a powerful phenomenon that implies the actions we model in the light and in the dark (Figure 6.1). I invited Michael to draw a sketch of his leadership shadow and the possible leadership behaviors that are being cascaded to frontline teams.

The shadow of the leader is evident in our parents and children. Whether you like it or not, we inherit behaviors we appreciate in our parents. We also inherit behaviors we do not appreciate. These behaviors show up in our lives consciously or unconsciously. The same goes for our children. We see behaviors in our children that we desire, as well as the ones we vehemently dislike in ourselves. Our actions speak louder than our words. What we say is overruled by what we do, at work and at home. We may lecture our kids about excessive use of their phones, and then they watch us use our phones until the late hours of the night. Our actions overshadow our words every time.

FIGURE 6.1. THE SHADOW OF THE LEADER

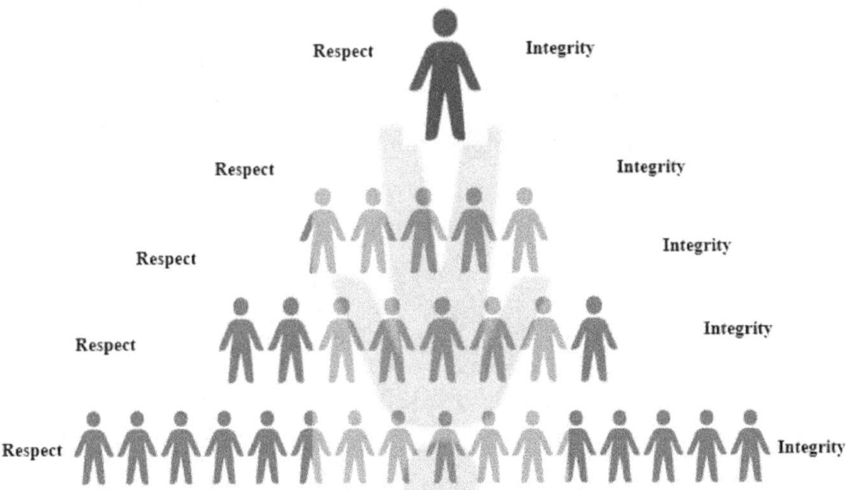

Our actions overshadow our words every time.

The Balancing Act

Middle managers are key drivers of humanity during change. Yet, they find themselves in a unique situation of being middle children. You are stuck in a social puzzle that requires continuous awareness and assimilation into the political and emotional games of navigating power.

Part of the challenge for middle managers is the expectation that you must be willing, excited, and unconditionally welcoming to take on more change. Resistance and grievances about the multitude of conflicting priorities hitting your overly crowded priority list are unacceptable. In fact, they are career derailers. You are expected to maintain a balance between assertive direction and interpersonal relationships. You must ace the art of embracing recurring changes to the change, while driving inspiration and order across your teams. You are expected to switch from a place of being highly *accommodating* when dealing with your managers to a place of *control and command* when dealing with your team.

This balancing act can be quite challenging for many middle managers. It feels inconsistent even to the most experienced ones. You often find yourself stuck between various stakeholder groups and relentless demands. You experience being the victim *and* the *enabler* of a top-down change strategy; you are the receiver on one side and the implementer on another. Under these demanding circumstances, when you are unable to voice your opinion or question the need to make the change, it can begin to feel like an attack against your personal well-being and dignity.

Middle managers have a complicated relationship with power because it is experienced within the context of interpersonal relationships. Shifting from a deferential position when interacting with their superiors, to then assuming a more assertive position when dealing with direct reports, can be tasking. They manage the expectations of two opposing stakeholder groups. The shift from agreeable to demanding is mentally demanding.

Middle managers play a critical role in influencing their teams to commit to a large change initiative. Here are some strategies you can employ:

1. **Communicate purpose:** Middle managers clarify the purpose and vision for change. They can act as facilitators of change conversations and evaluate change readiness and gaps within the organization.

2. **Model the way:** Middle managers inspire frontline teams to commit to the change by holding the space for intimate conversations and actively embracing the change so others follow suit.

3. **Address concerns:** Middle managers can acknowledge resistance among team members and take the time to validate their experiences during change. They can dedicate time and effort to empower their teams to problem-solve and design just-in-time interventions.

4. **Promote trust and collaboration:** Trust is a critical ingredient during change. Middle managers can design specific team interventions that promote trust and collaboration across disciplines. Providing the necessary support can improve collaboration and improve confidence in top leadership.

5. **Celebrate Progress:** Middle managers take time to celebrate milestones and achievements related to the change effort. No matter how small, acknowledging progress can improve morale and maintain momentum.

FIGURE 6.2. THE MULTIPLE ROLES OF MIDDLE MANAGEMENT

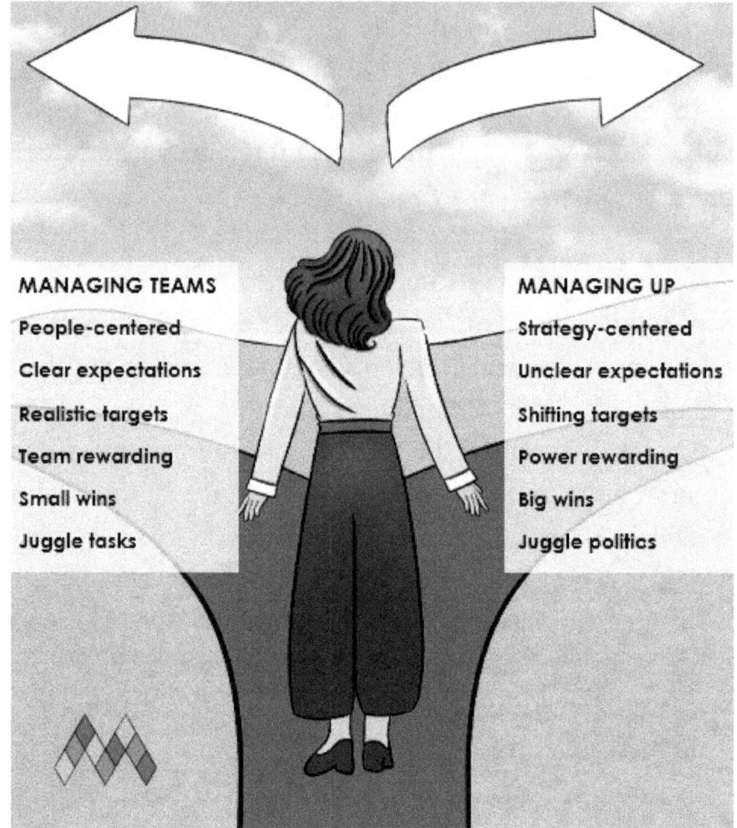

Making the shift from order-taker to commander is mentally demanding and tasking on middle managers.

Middle managers are super change commanders. They are counted on to make quick decisions about multi-faceted, long-term projects, from a distance, uninterrupted and unaware of conversations at the top and relentless interactions with day-to-day workers.

The role of the middle manager is critical during organizational change. On one hand, you are empowered with knowledge about the change, and on the other hand, your opinion is sidelined. You find pathways to collective intelligence, and you become *the* voice of reality for frontline staff. Your role cannot be silenced. You have the added responsibility of being the bearer of good or bad news. Being able to master your story and to share a more systematic sketch of the impact of the change is critical for you to mitigate failure during change.

The more rushed you feel, the bigger the need for you to pause and reassess the people side of change. Savvy executives who commit to the development of their managers can impact resilience during disruption. According to Korn Ferry, a global organizational research firm, how executives make decisions *warrants* an honest review. When it comes to urgent and complex change initiatives, some of the most overlooked individuals are middle managers. We must empower middle managers to influence the change effort. While executives spark inspiration for the vision for change, middle managers inspire the masses to action. They do so while artfully balancing daily deliverables and overarching deadlines.

> While executives spark inspiration for the vision for change, middle managers drive the masses to action.

Shifting from Blame to Empowerment

I was supporting Niran, an EVP for a large, higher-education system in Ohio, in leading a large system optimization. Niran expressed his frustration with his lead director, Diana, whom he described as overly stressed about the change to the new platform. He went on to emphasize that moving to a virtual learning platform was ideal, dictated by an escalating global student body. The challenge was real, and the shift to a virtual platform had to happen immediately.

When I met Diana, over lunch outside the office, she concurred. "The change is necessary. I am an igniter, a doer, and I have been talking about the need for this transformation for years. I don't have the resources to make it happen. I'm scared of losing my two key people. They are overstretched and underpaid. I don't have a magic wand. My boss expects a superb performance within four weeks, but my team is ready to quit." Niran's expectations were not aligned with Diana's reality. Diana was stuck between order-taking and therapy sessions with her team. She had lost a senior team member last month. When she complained to her manager, he minimized her fear and invited her to think outside the box. He believed in outsourcing, and she worried about the waste of time training a highly paid outsider. "My job is to make sure we have a box," Diana said. "We need the tools within the box to work seamlessly." Hiring a contractor was going to take four weeks and training a temporary worker was frustrating. Diane's obvious distress was not clear to Niran.

Diana understood too well the sense of urgency with the change. Her resistance was valid. She lacked the resources her team needed to deliver on time. She felt that Niran's drive for quick results prevented him from understanding the details and from validating her concerns. Diana was frustrated about the next difficult conversation with not only her manager but also her team. She would wake up at 3:00 a.m. worried about the next day. She was offered a job that would be less demanding, and she was considering it. She loved her job but the demand on her well-being was difficult to sustain. "Niran wants me to produce a state-of-the-art system with a weak foundation. There are only so many ways to screw the nail. We need time, not solutions. I know the solution." Diana gave up on talking to Niran. Instead, she defaulted to silence. "I beat myself up enough. I don't need my boss's help to do so."

Frustration and silence derail progress during change. Trusting your team propels it forward. Although misunderstandings are expected at times of change, they become dangerous when middle managers feel disrespected. The damage to a culture of trust is too high to ignore. I went back to Niran and advised him to listen to Diana with empathy and a sincere desire to understand her experience. She needed him to listen to her expertise so they could get better results. Without open and respectful communication, dissatisfaction can cascade through the culture. These symptoms of dysfunction will cause the change effort to fail.

Frustration and silence derail healthy change. Authentic conversations propel it forward.

Consider how much effort you have placed on creating an environment where people feel respected, included, and connected to a purpose. Consider how much importance you place on building social networks, meaningful connections, and informal feedback loops. People-centered models during change drive collaboration and creativity across divergent functions and propel them to solve complex problems *together*. Serendipity happens when people come together to innovate, create, and positively transform the work environment.

Case in Point—Feedback that Counts

A dear former colleague of mine invited me to support his company in developing a more flexible retention and succession-planning process. Jackie, the COO, shared her desire to create a more progressive process for hiring new leaders. Having a system-wide retention strategy would help her create a better leadership pipeline. "I am concerned about our first-year turnover rates. We train them and we lose them as quickly to our competitors. The cost and morale of my staff are concerning to me." It was clear to Jackie that money was not the issue.

Through discovery sessions with the senior leadership team, directors, managers, and staff, we learned that the annual performance review process had been the same for the past twelve years. Their internally designed system worked like clockwork, and about 90 percent of managers completed employee reviews on time. Due to more urgent client-facing priorities, an in-house design was considered sufficient to meet the company's needs. Feedback took place once a year, and every employee was placed on a three-point rating scale where 1 = you are the cream of the crop; 2 = you are good/okay; 3 = you need help. The maximum annual pay raise an exceptional employee could receive was 3.25 percent.

I asked Jennifer, a high-potential manager, about the last time she had a meaningful performance review with her employee. She admitted that she had not had a performance conversation with Kyle since the previous January. "Kyle is exceptional, and we get along well. I'm just too busy dealing with the day-to-day changes, and what am I going to say, anyway? 'Congratulations, Kyle, your pay raise for exceptional performance is less than the annual inflation rate? I understand your point about looking for a better-paying job?"

I told Jennifer that feedback matters. What if Kyle interpreted your lack of attention as a lack of interest in his development? What if Kyle was actively looking for a new role where he could grow and learn, and you might be able to engage in dialogue about career growth with him and retain him? Current research depicts that 87 percent of employees want to "be developed" on the job, but only a third report receiving the feedback they need to engage and improve.

Question 1: What could Jennifer do differently?

Question 2: What retention strategy would you recommend to Jackie?

Question 3: What is a potential opportunity to coach middle managers on?

Tools for Talking During Change

Tool 6.1—Become an Influencer of Change

You can choose to transition from an order-taker to an influencer of change. This transition is critical to your personal engagement. It can keep things in focus, resolve unplanned gaps, and prioritize what is important, not what is screaming "urgent."

Influencers of change adopt five key behaviors:

1. Establish a clear purpose for the change and share it with your peers and team.
2. Connect the dots for your team so they can clearly see, hear, and feel the end result.
3. Identify culture champions that promote reliable, comprehensive, and consistent communication across different levels of the organization.
4. Lead intentional dialogue that promotes collaboration and accountability.

Tool 6.2—Leadership Influence

Leadership and the power that comes with it makes us vulnerable to the traps of hubris and self-focus, which can erode our effectiveness and lead to a disconnect with our teams. By cultivating empathy, we improve job satisfaction and engagement. Former CEO of Xerox Anne Mulcahy was called "the master of 'I don't know'" by her team members. "They actually gain confidence in you when you admit you don't know something." Encourage participation by creating formal channels for honest input.

Humility takes self-awareness to the next level. It provides us with an accurate view of our own abilities and limitations. Consider using this brief survey to assess your self awareness and emotional

intelligence capability. As you consider the Emotional Intelligence*
attributes below, rank each on a scale of 1 to 5:

5 = Top-notch 4 = Good 3 = Fair 2 = It Depends 1 = Need Support

Emotional Intelligence Attributes		
	Inspiration	Do I articulate a compelling vision? Do I bring out the best in people?
	Empathy	Do I understand what motivates others? People from diverse backgrounds?
	Attunement	Do I listen attentively to his/her team? Am I sensitive to the feelings of the team?
	Influence	Do I persuade others by engaging them in discussion? Do I persuade others by appealing to their self-interest?
	Teamwork	Do I solicit input from everyone on the team? Do I encourage collaboration among the team?
	Organizational Awareness	Do I appreciate the culture and values of the group? Am I aware of the "unspoken rules" and norms?
	Developing Others	Do I mentor with compassion? Do I provide feedback that people find helpful?

Recommendation: Go a step further and share your answers to
your peers and trusted team members to gain a clearer view of your
leadership shadow and influence.

*Attribute definitions adapted from *HBR Social Intelligence and the Biology of
Leadership* by Daniel Goleman and Richard Boyatzis (2008).

Summary

Communicate the good, the bad, and the ugly.
1. Notice limiting beliefs and transform them into empowering thoughts.
2. Beware of the shadow of the leaders.
3. Empower your middle managers to own the change.
4. Practice empathy to promote trust.
5. Seek tools to support your personal development journey.

Why don't they just do what we tell them to do?
Is this a trick question?

Leadership Essential 5

Calibrate Your Results and Target Clear Outcomes

"Talent is the multiplier. The more energy and attention you invest in it, the greater the yield. The time you spend with your best is, quite simply, your most productive time."

~ MARCUS BUCKINGHAM

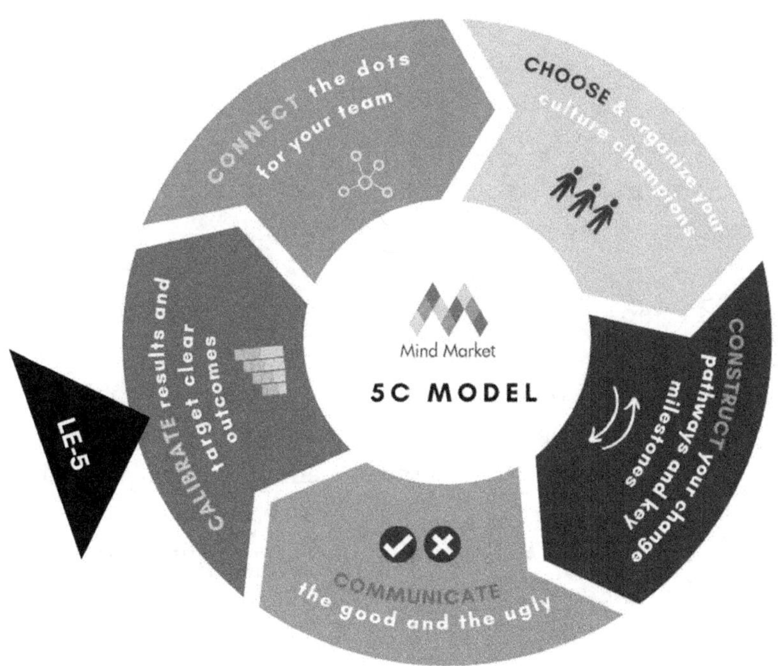

Start with the Highest Purpose for Change

Today's leaders are navigating a landscape filled with unprecedented challenges. They are facing economic uncertainties and global instability. To navigate and sustain targeted outcomes, leaders must communicate their goals and share results with *transparency*. A keen focus on priority calls for *reliable* internal communication channels that *prioritize* people, ensure their involvement in decision-making and convey their value to the change process. This alignment encourages your teams to challenge assumptions and confront superficial compliance. Tracking progress through outcome-based metrics helps your teams stay on course and encourages conversations regarding obstacles and competing priorities using dependable systems and structures.

People-centered change empowers leaders to nurture a culture that invests heavily in alignment, information flow, and cross-functional collaboration. Its leaders set realistic expectations and reinforce a higher purpose for change through everyday conversations. In a people-centered culture, managers are able to distinguish between *targeted goals* and reactive approaches to change. They anticipate blocks to progress and foster resilience in the face of setbacks. They work *across* functions to develop systems that measure clear outcomes and calibrate results on the go.

People-centered leaders capitalize on their talent to maintain a *growth* mindset. They recognize the importance of:

- Promoting well-being and preventing burnout for themselves and others
- Removing obstacles and red tape to enable problem-solving and decision-making across teams
- Empowering their teams to embrace a *curious* mindset and alternative ways of thinking
- Enabling a consistent emphasis on measuring and sharing clear outcomes

In short, people-centered change places *people* at the core of transformation. Its leaders realize that transformation is only possible when people commit to it and enable their peers to be actively engaged in transformation. Their focus on desired outcomes, coupled with effective team development, makes lasting change possible.

Target Efficiency and Clarity

Productivity and efficiency are paying the cost of emotional drain. The *busyness* syndrome has transformed into *agonizing* hours of unproductive meetings. To innovate, we must begin by transforming ourselves and coaching others to do the same. Managers constantly complain about the lack of efficiency in meetings, yet they hesitate to take *profound* measures to stop the waste of energy and collective intelligence.

Start by evaluating the busyness of your day and enabling your team to drive efficiency through new daily habits. Experts suggest the following practices:

- Reduce the number of meetings and unnecessary presentations during meetings.
- Limit the number of unproductive emails and team chats.
- Translate strategic plans into weekly priorities that have clear owners and time-bound deliverables.
- Encourage your team to identify and eliminate practices that stand in the way of them doing something better.
- Remove processes that do not align with your change strategy.
- Hold your team accountable for results. Get out of the way and calibrate as needed to stay on track.
- Raise awareness of collaboration across departments and functions.
- Design moments of celebrations and intentional acknowledgment of small wins.

Make your overarching goal so transparent that, at every level, employees are capable and willing to connect the dots about the change. When people connect to purpose, change becomes a personal mission. During a visit to the NASA Space Center in 1962, President Kennedy noticed a janitor carrying a broom. He interrupted his tour, walked over to the man, and said: "Hi, I'm John Kennedy. What are you doing?" The janitor responded: "I'm helping put a man on the moon, Mr. President." The janitor understood how his work contributed to the overarching goal of your organization. Make your outcomes so transparent that every person in the organization recognizes how they contribute to it. *Overcommunicate* your strategy and celebrate relevant milestones across the way.

Prep Your Talent for Transformation

Leadership and talent development are on every CEO's mind. The goal is to create a stream of ready-now leaders that are resilient and focused when stakes are high. The impact of change is felt when you elevate the culture through leadership behaviors and narratives that support transformation. Each team in your organization experiences culture differently. Team experiences are unique to their function, and they are hugely influenced by their individual leader. Culture is not consistent across all departments; it is felt differently by different teams.

Take for example International Insurance, a France-based company, whose culture nurtures one family, compassion, and respect for all. Most leaders in the company nurture the one-family value and promote compassion within their functions. Melanie, the VP of Technical Operations, is different. She is smart, hard working, assertive and controlling. She micromanages her team because of an intrinsic belief that every team member is incompetent. Melanie has a VP position and yet operates at the supervisor level. She takes full control of writing her department's Standard Operating Procedures and insists on training new team members using her incredibly complex, manually-created, operating manual. She works fifteen hours a day and prides herself on waking up at 3:00 a.m. to think about her to-do list.

"I cannot shut down; we have a lot to do and not enough time in the day," she explained to me with pride and agony. Melanie is highly regarded by the CEO and feared by her team. Her managers share stories about her toxic mood swings and impatience when teaching the team. She denigrates staff members that resign and labels them as incapable. She insists that most people on her team are taking advantage of her. While the CEO and his team are modeling and speaking transformation, Melanie's shadow stands against the flow.

It is our responsibility to ensure that our leaders align with the vision and values we set forth. The key to people-centered change begins with an intentional look at our culture and the leaders who support it. It calls for a non-negotiable commitment to promoting a people-centered approach to managing teams, including addressing toxic behaviors that get in the way of intended outcomes. Losing Melanie would create a significant knowledge gap for the company. However, relying on one sole expert to implement new technologies also puts the company at risk. I recommended that her role shift from a leader of people to leading the technical side of change, and to select a compassionate, people-centered leader to develop the team, and to help them identify high-potential members that the department can rely on to move the company in the right direction. I supported Melanie and her team through the transition. Four months later, the managers reported a 39% increase in client satisfaction and 33% improvement in product failure. More importantly, Melanie shared her relief from dealing with constant, strenuous relationships and her focus on what she does best led her to sustaining a zero-error environment for 193 days.

Team experiences are unique to each function, and are largely influenced by their individual leader.

When Google ran the "experiment" that led to getting rid of all functional managers, the purpose of the change was *operational autonomy*; that is, letting go of one extra layer of bureaucracy and helping people make better decisions across functions. It made sense at the time. In hindsight, Google researchers realized the gravity of their decision. It was a mistake. These layers of management that once were thought to create bottlenecks and waste were the very same layers that mattered the most.

As a result, Google took a spin on things and focused instead on making these managers the best at their game. Their focus shifted to exploring what makes a great manager at Google. "Project Oxygen" was born with the mission to identify what the best managers at Google look, sound, and feel like. Their findings became the roadmap for their leadership development programs. The real shift happened when Google focused on helping managers get better at what they do, instead of blaming them for where they are in their development journey. New and seasoned managers became more equipped to show up as better coaches, collaborators, decision-makers, and communicators. They transformed to people-centered, vision-focused, and results-oriented.

We are constantly focused on what is going wrong, and our relentless attention to what the next crisis may be is draining. We may not have the answers to everything. However, we can enable our managers to refocus on the vision for change and elevating others through people-centered practices. We can coach them to identify key milestones, celebrate progress consistently, and recognize the unsung heroes in their change efforts. Current research on leadership competencies reveals that two potential competencies where leaders struggle the most are developing others and recognizing others. These two competencies are critical to propel managers to become enablers of change so as to have a significant impact on results.

Given the challenges many client-facing organizations are grappling with, you can pave the way for managers to develop and master change leadership skills that drive commitment to change far beyond the urgent stages. People-centered practices can help you sustain change over time.

Develop Them or Watch Them Leave

A prominent factor during change is retaining capable people to implement and sustain the change effort. Microsoft's Work Trend Index Special Report depicts that the current workforce will leave unless you have plans in place to develop their skills and help them grow professionally. A Microsoft survey with 20,000 employees show that 64 percent of Gen Zs and Millennials as well as 60 percent of Gen Xers believe that the best way to develop their skills is by changing companies. Innovations like self-driving vehicles, artificial intelligence, and instant content-creation tools are reshaping the way we do work. As a result, training your leaders to engage their teams to stay committed to learn and transform the way they operate can help companies mitigate the technological disruptions that continue to challenge current business models.

FIGURE 7.1. DEVELOP THEM TO STAY

Help them grow or watch them leave

Most workers believe that they need to change companies to develop their skills.

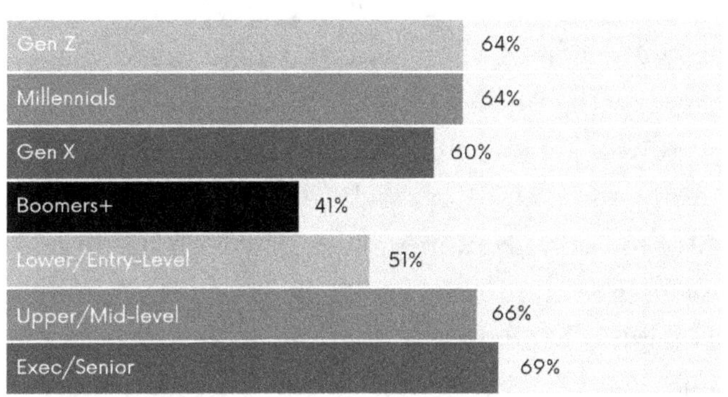

Every generation in the workplace, including upper and middle management, expects to learn and grow, or leave (Figure 7.1). Inviting the team to problem solve and make informed decisions can nurture awareness, alignment, and trust in the process. The emerging dialogue creates a pathway to ideal outcomes. Elevate your power and empower others to take ownership of the metrics that define their day-to-day outcomes.

Change Leadership

In our research with managers, four recurring themes stood out amid the myriad stories regarding mammoth change efforts. This change leadership competency model summarizes the skills that promote a people-centered change culture (See figure 7.2). The model is designed to inform leadership development and coaching programs that are designed to drive lasting change.

The opportunity to develop managers and culture champions is of paramount importance. The skills can prepare the managers to communicate with influence, inspire people to commit, and drive change with more resilience and less resistance. Change is relentless and elevating managers to drive change through people is your best bet to sustain your change initiative beyond takeoff.

Putting thousands of managers through leadership development programs can be expensive. The challenge is avoiding the waste of over-the-counter training solutions to facilitate growth. Designing a program that fits the needs of your culture is of critical essence. Shortchanging learning with one-size-fits-all training solutions is like throwing darts toward our target with our eyes closed. Developing managers requires a more strategic approach so you align the investment to the strategy of the organization and design your milestones in a way that effectively uses team intelligence to avoid the crash.

The Change Leadership Model we propose (Figure 7.2) includes four quadrants of leadership competencies that we identified as fundamental contributors to a people-centered leader. While numerous change management programs prioritize the process aspects of change, our methodology places a *premium* on leadership principles and skills tailored to engage the people dimension—the arena where *alignment* and *conflicts* surrounding change arise among stakeholders.

The task of managing and sustaining change within organizations is both complex and demanding. Consider, for example, project managers like Lean Six Sigma practitioners, who spearhead organizational changes across multiple departments. These individuals serve as change catalysts within their organizations. Research indicates that a notable portion (62 percent) of Lean Six Sigma project change initiatives fail, often due to a *disregard* for the people aspect of change and an excessive focus on procedural elements. Overall, project leaders dedicate 88 percent of their time to interacting with various stakeholders and engaging in conversations while implementing projects. The absence of social and emotional skills, detrimentally impacts project success.

Scholars argue that change agents with heightened emotional intelligence are better equipped to navigate successful change endeavors. The emotional intelligence of these change agents positively influences employees' attitudes toward change. A recent study conducted by Dr. Y. Gokalp uncovered no substantial disparity in emotional intelligence traits between 225 Black Belt Lean Six Sigma (LSS) practitioners who underwent the LSS program and those who did not. This finding shows that conventional project management training often fails to adequately equip practitioners with the skills needed to effectively engage and persuade others in the critical aspects of enduring change efforts. While conventional project management methods may prepare participants for the 22 percent of their time spent on technical tasks, they often fall short in addressing the 88 percent portion dedicated to engaging with change stakeholders. Our model supports participants in crafting people-centered practices during change. Coaching in organizations is underrated as it pertains to managing complex change. It is an essential element in helping leaders focus on people-centered practices when they matter most.

FIGURE 7.2. MIND MARKET'S CHANGE LEADERSHIP COMPETENCIES©

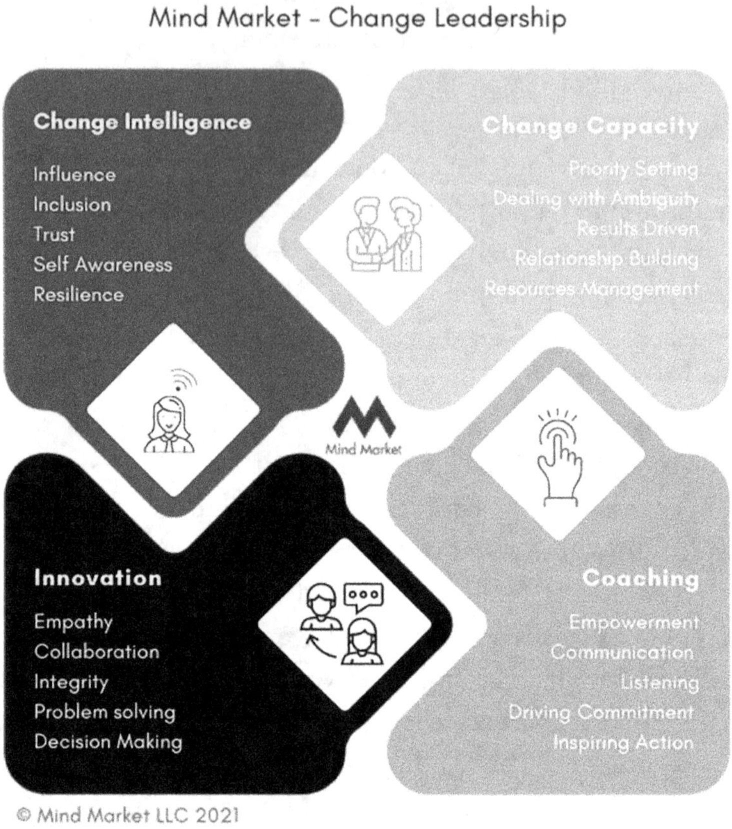

Leadership Capability for Change

The four leadership pillars for change include the following competencies and skills that require more focus to help managers thrive during change:

I. Change Intelligence is about making managers more aware of their shadow of influence during change. It is about creating the intention for managers to promote psychological safety and empathy as high-potential teams experience transitions from loss of what *is* to the possibilities of what *could be*.

- **Self-Awareness.** The ability to understand one's personal strengths, liabilities, stressors, and motivators is critical to leadership influence during times of change. The leader must show a clear commitment to learning and continuous self-improvement for this competency to enact healthy change.
- **Resilience.** Setbacks are unavoidable during change. The demand to do more work can stretch managers beyond their capabilities. Being *resilient* means keeping a positive attitude amid all that could and does go wrong. It also means staying focused and composed under high pressure.
- **Psychological Safety.** When managers promote psychological safety, they allow high-potential teams to thrive through creativity, risk-taking, speaking their minds, and being vulnerable without fear of criticism, blame, or punishment. Nurturing an environment of safety requires intentional conversations and behaviors every single day.
- **Empathy.** *Empathy* starts with self-compassion and reaches toward understanding the perspectives of others. When managers can express positive feelings and affinity toward others, they promote feelings of dignity, connections, and belonging among their teams and peers.
- **Trust.** When there is trust between the manager and the team, the sky's the limit. By modeling high standards of honesty, integrity, and dignity, and when teams know that their managers have their back, trust begins to illuminate the path toward commitment and engagement.

II. Change Capacity is the ability to navigate change using best practices and tools that support the execution of change in a specific and accurate manner. It focuses on the processes and activities necessary to get the masses to implement and sustain the change effort.

- **Priority Setting.** Leaders perceive what is necessary to be accomplished and act accordingly. They understand what tasks align to the vision and goals of the change, and identify blocks to progress, including what needs to stop, in a timely and efficient manner.

- **Relationship Building.** In organizations, *relationship building* is the energy that can transform desired results into tangible outcomes. It is the superpower that propels teams to want to support each other beyond the boundaries of work. By being diplomatic, approachable, and friendly, managers become catalysts of change.

- **Dealing with Ambiguity.** Today's managers are faced with global disruptions in the digital, mental, and medical spaces. The art of making decisions comfortably during ferocious change is not an easy task. It requires the ability to cultivate and recalibrate operations and scale them to the next level with what resources are available at hand.

- **Resources Management.** Understanding and aligning resources to impact results requires a clear understanding of how every resource allocation impacts overall operations and conflicting priorities. Knowing how to organize and simplify work in an efficient manner is an essential element in change. This also means avoiding reworking processes unnecessarily by bringing processes together through a holistic approach that takes into consideration aspects of time, budget, quality, safety, and continuous improvement.

- **Results Driven.** Leaders create a sense of urgency and have a strong focus on bottom-line outcomes that can make or break the cycle of change. Driving results is about creating the vision for change, communicating the vision for change, and focusing on the drivers of change that can mitigate roadblocks for the team.

III. Coaching. New times call for new ways to manage. The manager as a coach is no longer "nice to have." It is the way for managers to engage and influence their teams during change. The manager-coach asks questions to gauge interest and insight within their teams. They promote exploration in place of command and control and provide support to help their teams uncover blocks and adapt to a constantly changing environment.

- **Listening.** Most managers rate themselves much higher on this competency than their peers or direct reports would. It is a blind spot that gets a lot of attention and little action. Listening is your doorway to innovation. When you listen with curiosity, you show a sincere willingness to understand the other person. The pause is a powerful component of listening. The manager can validate the opinions of others and make sure they feel heard before responding to what is initially said.

- **Communication.** The manager delivers messages in a clear, compelling, and consistent manner. Through open dialogue and intentional conversations, the manager uses diplomacy and tact to articulate the purpose and dynamics of change while understanding the fears of others.

- **Empowerment.** The sense of empowerment during change can directly impact employee commitment and determination in the change effort. The manager takes into consideration the input of others while planning change and makes sure that the contributions of the team are visible and valued. The manager encourages the team to participate in problem-solving and decision-making during change.

- **Inspiring Action.** An essential part of change is to promote a sense of urgency to make the change happen. This means compelling key stakeholders to take action and to engage in change. It also means building strong advocacy around change milestones and success drivers for the long-term benefits of change. Inspiring action starts with a keen focus on the *why* to get to the *how*.
- **Inspiring Commitment.** The simple act of being present and paying positive attention can drive the team to want to commit to the change effort. The manager must start with appreciation and understanding of the power of commitment during the change. Silence is not agreement. Resistance can lead to failure in many aspects of change.

IV. Innovation. Companies that squelch innovation can no longer compete with companies that champion innovation. New players got to where they are by being nimble, creative, and relentless about a client-centered approach to change. The client experience must align with an exceptional employee experience. Organizations must innovate to thrive and excel in a highly competitive and ever-changing environment. The stories of Blockbuster and Netflix are great reminders of what *was* versus what *could be possible*. It is about constantly looking for possibilities, harnessing research and evidence-based practices to rethink the way you do business.

- **Problem Solving.** The manager can make connections among related and unrelated drivers of change. She or he harnesses the power of the team to scrutinize potential difficulties and opportunities. The manager can identify the root cause of the problem using simple tools that everyone understands and contributes to. Google engineers are encouraged to take 20 percent of their time to work on something that they are personally interested in being part of. That can be part of any change management process.

- **Decision-Making.** Making good judgments and feeling confident about your decision-making can be quite challenging when the stakes are high, and the tides of change are never-ending. As such, making quality decisions when you don't have a full picture or all the data to support your decision can be quite tasking. Skillfully separating facts from fiction and inviting the team to share challenges and possibilities requires confidence, patience, and trust.
- **Integrity.** Integrity is a deal-breaker during change. It takes humility and courage to be candid. Articulating your values is not enough. Telling is not enough. Modeling these values in a consistent manner during change is critical to driving the change effort. The shadow of a leader can cascade throughout the organization and promote integrity, or it can cascade through leadership behaviors that misalign with the mission, vision, and values of the organization. Employees who receive an unethical request at work may feel trapped. When they comply with the request, their behavior may lead to feelings of guilt or regret.
- **Collaboration.** Promoting collaboration across disciplines is an essential leadership trait during change. Cutting through the walls of silos can bring about effective change where teams collaborate to get better results. FedEx24 is a great example of such collaboration. Teams are invited to reshape the way they do work and harness the power of specialized teams to collaborate and work together to accomplish goals during change.
- **Cohesion.** Cohesion is about being the glue that brings teams together. It is intentional. It is not accidental. It is nurtured through breakthrough dialogue and a keen awareness of the purpose of change. Teams perform at

their best when they have common measures for success and rally behind common goals. Competitive measures for performance can derail highly effective teams during change.

With newfound clarity, confidence, and determination, your talent will be determined to empowering others, driving positive change through a legacy of trust, passion, and accountability. In the fast-paced landscape of businesses today, effective leadership is not merely a skill; it's a form of art that requires nurturing, constant refinement, and drive. Developing your talent to drive change can revolutionize the way you empower everyone around you to believe and commit to your vision. People-centered change involves intention, capability, and willingness to believe in the collective intelligence of your people. Without it, you become painfully reliant on the brilliance of the few to drive your results. People-centered change invites everyone to want to be part of your transformation journey.

"If you think education is expensive, try ignorance."
Unknown

Case in Point—Because I Said So

When I first met Sebastian, a world-renowned surgeon, he was visibly offended at the results of a recent employee engagement survey that ranked him poorly across team motivation and personal interactions. As head of a large healthcare organization, he was accustomed to dealing with crises but was not prepared to accept being assigned a leadership coach or to make changes in how he managed his team. During our first meeting, he proudly and assertively described his leadership style as one that required direct and firm adherence to operational standards and budget constraints. "My communications with my team are clear and no-nonsense. I don't have time to coddle people. They are here to do a job and I expect them to do it." In short, Sebastian was operating from a restrictive definition of leadership—command and control.

When asked to describe Sebastian, his direct reports gave examples of how oblivious he was to how often he demeaned others. They commented on his bursts of anger and impatience. His tendency to lash out at them was a common theme. When he initially heard what others thought of his behavior, he became quite defensive. Sebastian didn't know what he didn't know. You can't work on a problem you don't understand. As he accepted the feedback, he became more self-aware, and he was slowly able to realize the negative impact his words and actions had on the team.

1. How would you describe a "psychologically safe" team environment?
2. How would you coach Sebastian to be an influencer of change?
3. How can a leader inspire others to drive change?

People-centered leadership is not necessarily about having all the answers; it is about inspiring others to *own* the process and take the lead, regardless of their role or rank in an organization. Sebastian had to redefine his role as leader and build the skills necessary to earn the trust of his team.

Enable change by learning the skills needed to influence others to want to commit and engage in the change effort. As Sebastian began to listen, he went beyond his comfort zone and allowed his team leaders to create a psychologically safe environment that led to enhanced collaboration when determining priorities and critical milestones. This empowering approach created the pathways for growing the operating room into a giant, nationally accredited, multi-regional system.

Good intentions can easily get lost when we *degrade* the people experience during change. Better's CEO, Vishal Garg, decided to inform over 900 employees that they were being terminated, on a Zoom webinar, right before the holidays. Garg said, "If you're on this call, you are part of the unlucky group that is being laid off." The CEO explained that the decision behind the firing of so many employees was due to market efficiency, performance, and productivity. Unfortunately, among those fired were the diversity, equity, and inclusion recruiting team. One of those employees, Christian Chapman, said that at the end of the three-minute call, her computer turned off. "I was cut off from people I knew for years. I have been unceremoniously laid off. Already working from home by myself, the isolation was numbing." Better's actions created a worldwide focus on the importance of humanity during change.

Two months later, Bettter.com laid off an additional 3,000 employees (one-third of the workforce). Trying to avert the recent fallout from disgruntled employees, they took a more positive approach and decided to have one-on-one conversations with each member. Unfortunately, many of those employees learned of their fate because their severance pay had been deposited *before* the calls to inform them of their termination. Rushed communication has a price. The constant rush can cause unintended outcomes that can be avoidable.

Tools for Talking During Change

Tool 7.1—Improve the Gap Between Intent and Impact

Sebastian, the well-known surgeon we discussed, was focused on productivity, not on team engagement. During coaching, we identified examples of what he said, and because of the low-trust environment, how the team interpreted his message:

- What Sebastian said: "At the end of the day, it's all about getting the work done."

- What his team heard: "All I care about are the results, and if some are offended along the way, so be it."
- What Sebastian said: "If I can understand it, anyone can."
- What his team heard: "You're not smart enough to get this."
- What Sebastian said: "I don't see what the big deal is."
- What his team heard: "I don't really care how you feel."

It's almost impossible to communicate something clearly and succinctly to everyone all the time. So, misunderstandings occur. We misunderstand a comment or a gesture. Then what happens? When we talk with someone we like or trust, we give them the benefit of the doubt, even when they make mistakes. We assume that what they meant was aligned with who we believe they are. When we communicate with someone we don't trust, we often assume the worst. The challenge is to earn their trust; their benefit of the doubt.

Summary

The four competencies for people-centered change leaders are:
1. Change intelligence
2. Change capacity
3. Coaching
4. Innovation

Let's invest in more technology!
How about we start with how to be human?

The Five Leadership Essentials Connected

"You cannot hope to build a better world without improving the individuals. Each of us work for his own improvement and at the same time share a general responsibility for all humanity, our particular duty being to aid those to whom we think we can be most useful."

~ MARIE CURIE

Where Do We Go from Here?

The 5C Change Model is a culmination of the elements we consider essential to people-centered change. It brings together five keys that will support your journey to lead change that lasts. We start with the premise that people do not care how much you know until they know how much you care. Trust comes first on the journey to elevating leadership.

We ask ourselves: How can we build a community of talented people who are determined to change? How do we get there fast enough to create impact? How do we bridge the gap and humanize the change process?

Technology is accelerating at a pace that is beyond our imagination. The more dominant technology becomes, the more significant the people element. High-tech without high-touch is a recipe for disaster. Ethics and emotional intelligence are non-negotiable for our survival. In a rapidly evolving landscape, people-centered change isn't just essential; it's an urgent imperative. This holds particularly true as new technologies continue to expand the realm of possibilities. In essence, we want better leaders who can lead us through disruption.

As you explore the five leadership essentials summarized in this chapter, decide what key leadership essential you want to explore further with your team. Start with small steps that will help you create determined champions for change. Lead with the intention to overcommunicate your change vision. Select from the menu of practical tools we offer you in each chapter, one practice that will best serve your change journey. Design your people-centered change on the premise of one vision for change and a strong foundation of a people-centered strategy for change. Elevate your leadership so that purpose guides your conversations and humanity makes it happen.

FIGURE 8.1. THE 5-C CHANGE LEADERSHIP MODEL©

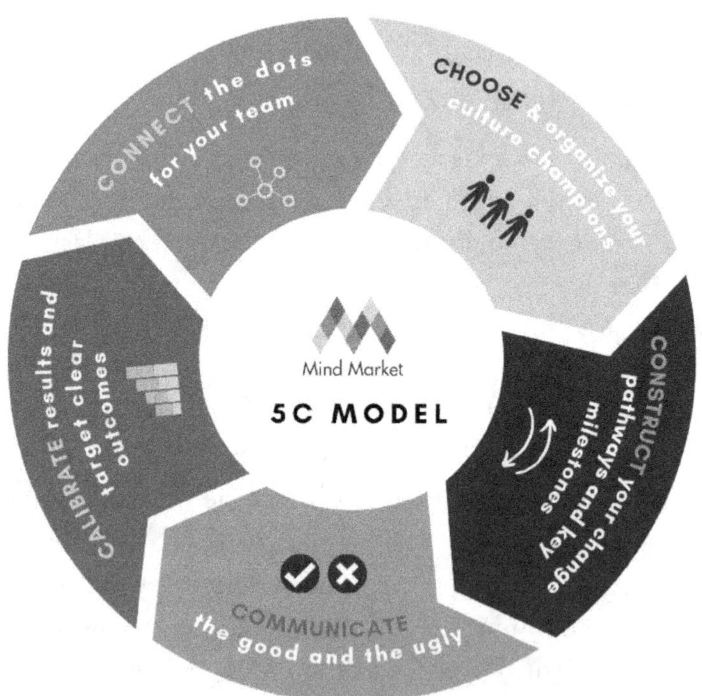

Connect the Dots for You and Your Team

Have a clear understanding of what your vision is and share it *consistently*. Understand the higher purpose, overcommunicate it, and draw a roadmap of the future that your teams can relate to. Hold change conversations with all levels of employees and listen to understand their fears during the initial phases of the change effort.

Start strong by nurturing a people-centered culture. Help your team accept mistakes as an opportunity to learn. Mitigate culture sharks who use the opportunity to shine, blame, or punish. Find a way to hardwire creativity and collaboration into your daily conversations with others. When this becomes your priority, you allow confusion to dissipate. Connecting the dots during change can be your biggest opportunity when you are pressured to deliver results and your urgency takes over your priority.

According to 2023 research by McKinsey, high-performing companies call for senior executives to *serve* as role models for creativity and innovation. You don't tell people to innovate; you model the behaviors to anchor these practices within your team. Almost 60 percent of top-performing executives self-identify as innovation leaders. The question is, are those same leaders perceived as innovation leaders by their teams?

Connect the dots *through* them, not *for* them. Provide permission for team members to challenge the vision and offer improbable pathways. Invite them to the table and empower them to co-create possibilities with you. Consider obstacles and competing priorities. Beware of superficial compliance. India's surge of COVID cases was spurred by scientists and medical teams who feared retaliation by their top leaders. Clarify, share, and develop your managers on how to communicate what you want to accomplish. Inspire examples and narratives that help people connect the dots.

I am currently supporting an organization that has witnessed significant turnover in the past six months. An intentional walk through some of the units followed by conversations with staff highlighted some of the challenges they face. We asked Jackie, the CNO, about her insights regarding our findings, and she completely agreed with us. She has been busy putting out fires and secretly hoped these problems would take care of themselves. When we asked her why she did not ask for help or bring it up to her peers, her response was: "Our culture is one thing; what we experience is another. I learned early on to stay quiet and fix my problems. I was hired with a clear message to think on my feet." Why not ask your team for help? Why not connect the dots for your team and let them transpire problems into *lasting* solutions?

Connect the dots through them, not for them.

Choose and Organize Your Culture Champions

Change necessitates forming strong partnerships and selecting the right champions to lead the change initiative. Involve your managers *before* the launch. Develop your frontline managers so they become instrumental in influencing the change effort. When you commit to change, you commit to drive home what matters to make the change last. Select culture champions who are credible, ethical, and committed to your culture.

Choose champions that people perceive as *positive* models for the organization. Culture champions are influencers of change. They are authentic, well respected, and capable of connecting with others and articulating the urgency for change. Instead of imposing their thoughts and ideas, champions invite others to *contribute* and to be *curious* about the opportunity for change. Curiosity sparks possibilities, and most often, the *determination* to change comes from an unlikely source.

Can one person make a difference? No doubt. A high school student in Phoenix, Arizona did just that. As part of her "Basha Gives

Back" senior service project, Jadyn Ocampo, along with her mother Sara Ocampo, came up with the idea to help teachers pay off some of their student loans. Jadyn understood the need as she represented the third generation of teachers in her family. She started with the goal of giving one teacher $1,000 using a fundraising site. She managed to raise far more, allowing her to grant three $1,000 scholarships and four $300 scholarships. Jadyn said, "Every time someone donated, I was like, 'Okay, I can help another person.'" With balloons and a large poster-sized check, she and her mother would knock on the classroom door and announce to the teacher, "I'm so happy to tell you, you are a recipient of the Al and Lori Ocampo Scholarship." Among cheers from the students and tears from the delighted teachers, Jadyn made a difference and found herself and her service project featured on *NBC News* in early 2022.

Champions *build the path* to humanity during change. Often, purpose gets distorted during takeoff. Champions communicate it through simple, daily narratives that help people connect to the purpose of change. We must involve employees at the onset of change to inspire collaboration and creativity during change. When Amazon invited its frontline employees to help improve the business, Charlie Ward, a software engineer, suggested the idea of free shipping, which became the unforeseen success behind Amazon Prime. Innovation *disguises* in the imagination of talented employees who are waiting to be tapped.

Start Strong: Develop your managers as champions of change and create diverse, cross-functional teams that construct the boundaries of change. Spark innovation through open dialogue about new possibilities that elevate your team to focus on an impeccable purpose.

Tipping Point: Be deliberate about designing a people-centered culture. When people believe in you, when you speak to their heart, you build determination far beyond your imagination. Connect to their heart, build strong relationships, and normalize the networks they create so you transform your organization with a greater sense of resilience. Evidence shows that supportive peer interactions improve the way employees manage day-to-day outcomes. Positive relationships at work are good for the bottom line. Happier, healthier employees are also less likely to "hide" (call out sick), incur high medical insurance costs, and become idea talent stallers.

> Innovation hides in the minds of talented employees who are waiting to be seen.

Construct Your Change Pathways and Key Milestones

Empower your team to co-create clear, specific, *mini* pathways for success. Identify weekly deliverables that help the team stay focused on progress. This process overrides the sense of overwhelm that teams encounter when unexpected complications impact the whole project. Your team will focus on weekly progress and mitigate the unnecessary rework associated with complex deliverables. Rework is expected during change, yet it causes major distress when the rework effort is immense. Focusing on mini milestones allows the team to stay focused on short and specific outcomes. Uncertainty erodes trust in the team's ability to achieve results.

Make time to discuss conflicting priorities among your team and remove *unnecessary* obstacles for good. *Conflicting* priorities derail progress and can consume your employees with a sense of resignation. This is particularly challenging for frontline managers who may be less enthusiastic about change and are tasked with driving more change through others. Enabling your managers to share their thoughts and challenges will serve the change effort in the long run.

Taking a well-timed pause, when you are overwhelmed, is one of the best time-management tools for reducing uncertainty—yours and those of everyone around you.

Communicate the Good and the Ugly

Communication is by far the *most* challenging component during change. Leaders whom we support admit that communication is ambiguous. The question is: What do employees need to be successful during change? Most senior leaders agree that holding change conversations is necessary. Finding the time to make it happen is the challenge. Crisis *demands* attention, and competing priorities can stifle the drive for change. Communication becomes less efficient when it hinders progress. As a result, you communicate less. This leads to employees feeling confused, frustrated, and inundated with tasks they perceive as a hindrance rather than an enhancement of their work.

Rather than spending weeks designing and crafting the right message, consider introducing "just-in-time" communication tools that are transparent and *straight to the point*. Place more emphasis on creating *adaptive* networks that are reliable and repeatable. Conducting "daily huddles" is one example of a simple and practical tool for promoting team communication during change. Train your managers and culture champions to conduct daily huddles with *intention* and sincere moments of *appreciation*. Other effective tools are available and are used by managers across the globe. What matters is to be able to have a constant stream of transparent and timely communication.

Focus on transparency and empathy and watch your employees accomplish the results.

Change is inevitable. A *flaky* change effort falls on middle managers to pay the price. This calls for a significant stretch in our ability to manage our well-being and your capacity to drive personal and team resilience. To be a successful advocate of change, each of us must learn to adapt, and often. We continue to embark on new journeys and deal with new challenges that we have not dealt with before.

Do not underestimate the *power* of communication at times of change. Linda Stone, a technology thought leader, says, "Attention is the most powerful tool of the human spirit. We can enhance or augment our attention with practices like meditation and exercise, diffuse it with technologies like email, texts, and social media, or alter it with pharmaceuticals. In the end, though, we are fully responsible for how we choose to use this extraordinary tool."

It is difficult to give 100 percent of our attention to human connections when our brain is racing against time-sensitive deliverables. The rush of speed and stress impedes our ability to *connect* for *meaning*. Being on the phone or reading emails while the team is trying to have a conversation with you is not an effective way to communicate understanding, let alone respect.

Calibrate Results and Target Clear Outcomes

Many change ideas start with a purpose. We lose track of purpose as we feel rushed and get bogged down with crisis. When your team understands the destination, it becomes easier for everyone to focus on achieving their individual accountability. It becomes easier to make decisions regarding what aligns, what to adopt, and what needs to go. When the pathways for success are explicit, your team recognizes what they need to stop doing and start doing. There is no substitute for advocating for the right goals and letting go of what is no longer necessary.

Switch from an action-based to a results-based mindset. This means calibrating *every* decision made based on whether it *supports the purpose* and outcome of the change effort. Communicate clear milestones and plan moments to celebrate small wins and course-correct unintended actions. Allow teams the *autonomy* to make decisions and pay specific attention to building connections that promote trust and empower *positive* connections. More importantly, measure results and report progress in a transparent and consistent manner.

Lasting culture change requires simple yet practical actions to drive consistent outcomes. Put people at the *center* of what you do; empower them to own the change. Through collaborative cultures you promote cohesive teams and mitigate culture sharks. Everyone is susceptible to irrational decision-making at times of constant change. Take time to communicate with purpose. Focus on the *people side*, and target *meaning* in outcomes to sustain the change. The challenge is not in the process. The hard work is instilling humanity and dignity into the process of change.

We lose track of purpose when we feel rushed and bogged down with crisis.

Inside Out (again)

I once woke up to the sound of guns right in front of my bedroom. I was ten years old. Sierra Leone was on the edge of civil war, and when there's an impending battle at your doorstep, you're likely to get some early, unwelcome visitors.

My family and I managed to flee into the darkness—the life we had (along with my coveted teddy bear) were left behind.

Change can come suddenly. And other people's agendas rarely have concerns for what you hold dear.

And this was just my first civil war. The second was in Lebanon while attending school. Weird isn't it that school happens while bombs detonate in the distant neighborhoods. During war, it become quickly obvious that living for the day is the only form of sanity. You feel untouchable, the guilt of surviving your friends and neighbors quickly replaced with unreal resilience.

Human beings are very adaptable. Which is a useful quality. But often we need to stop and question what it is we're adapting to.

These were difficult times. But eventually, I made my way to Canada as a refugee *against my family's wishes*.

And as someone who ultimately earned a doctorate in organizational leadership, spent over 20 years in corporate, and who now consults outside of it, what I can't help but notice is this: People speak strongly about world peace, yet they tend to choose war over peace at work.

Choose peace, not war. Choose peace in your dialogue with yourself, your family, your peers and your teams. Choose humanity so everyone can experience dignity in their lives.

You can only demand compliance from your people for so long. And **retaliation** comes in three different forms—**Escape** (employees quit). **Clash** (they develop and fight for their own agenda). **Hide** (they do the minimum and stay out of trouble).

Organizations with the most noble agenda can create the most *toxic* environments. And just because a new project is "successful" on paper, it doesn't mean in-house talent hasn't been suppressed. And that company *loyalty* hasn't been destroyed in the midst of too much rapid, mindless change.

Trust me, if you want to waste potential, put people in a situation where they spend their energy surviving instead of engaging their talents and contributing to strong cultures that sustain and run on united purpose.

I have witnessed fear replace a culture of transparency. I have watched people retreat to silence over speaking their truth. Losing your job is personal—it means a risk of losing your home, your dignity. The lack of control people experience during mergers and layoffs is similar to my experience with war. Fear is debilitating. Feeling unsafe at work is life consuming. It impacts your health, your confidence, your wellbeing, and your family.

No matter what conflicts arise on your path—**you and your team are so much more than your survival skills**. You are not just leading a team, you are influencing the experiences of hundreds, if not thousands, of people.

Change can disrupt our lives for the best or for the worst. Choose to elevate your leadership. Choose to win their hearts so you can inspire change for the better. Inspire change. Inspire your teams.

Loubna

Acknowledgements

Determined to Change is rooted in a decades-long conversation about leaders who impacted our lives through simple connections—moments so profound that they change how you think and behave. You remember these moments and share them with others. These human moments continue to live through our network of clients, associates and peers who have been generous enough to take our ideas, put them to the test and share their results with us. We owe a debt of gratitude to our family, friends and colleagues whose compassion, faith and 'yes and' ideas made sure we stayed on course.

Having someone who believes in you and supports you unconditionally even when you doubt yourself is a precious gift that keeps giving. I owe that to Janet Bell Taylor, my rock. We wanted to write a book about courageous moments and the book took us on a path to people-centered change. Janet is no longer with us, yet her unconditional love and voice keeps me determined to move forward.

We have a strong family bond that shows up strong in good times, and much stronger in hard times. We owe our deep gratitude to my sister Darine. You patiently read each chapter of the book, insisting on one more review. Thank you for believing in us and for your sincere commitment to our success. You helped us shift from a place of 'chaos to certainty.' We are your biggest fan.

We owe a lot to my niece Rasha. You patiently devoted your time to design many of the models and multiple cover concepts for the book. You were right there with us, from the very start. Your creative mind is an inspiration to us. Brilliant is an understatement when it comes to you.

A very special thanks to my daughter, Yara, my hope. Thank you for your generosity and patience as you transformed our concepts into graphics that we loved. Your support is priceless. You are one of a kind. Your thoughtfulness inspires me to want to be the best version of myself.

We are grateful for those who elevated our spirits by simply believing in us. I am deeply grateful to my husband Ziad, my daughter Jana, my joy, and my mom for the "You got this" attitude throughout this journey. Dad, you are my biggest fan and inspiration. I know you are watching me with your heart-warming smile from the other side.

A special thanks to our friend and advisor Nance Guilmartin who kept us honest in the telling of our stories and in staying true to the heart of people-centered change.

Scott Gallimore, your brilliant mind encouraged us to remember that "change happens as we write our book on change". Your kind and empathetic feedback helped us be more intentional in our message.

We are lucky to be surrounded with exceptional artists. We thank Ghina Fawaz for the creative, hand-drawn cartoon figures she designed for our book. You have a precious gift and we wish you all the best as you graduate from Columbia University.

Our thanks to the editorial expertise of Madalyn Stone and David Aretha. A sincere thank you to our book coach Martha Bullen for her guidance and insights into the world of publishing. We are grateful for her collaboration with our book designer, Christy Day, who remained dedicated to this project in spite of our many 'out of the box' and 'how about this?' ideas.

A deep thanks to my special writing group. Our accidental friendship and daily mindset meetings fill my heart with gratitude, encouragement, authenticity, humility, and laughter. I am a better writer because of you.

We thank our community of clients, mentors, and colleagues that we consider part of our family. We thank you for contributing your stories, experiences, and ideas.

A sincere thank you to our advance readers for your generosity with time and feedback. This book is better because of you.

We want to take a moment to thank you, our readers. Without you the concepts in this book will be silenced. Thank you for empowering humanity during change.

References

Chapter One

1. Noureddin, L. Enabling Organizational Change: How First-level Managers Influence and Commit to Implementing and Sustaining Change in a Healthcare System, Dissertation, Grand Canyon University, 2018

2. Gallup research cited in Dhingra, Samo, Schaninger & Schrimper, "Help Your Employees Find Purpose—Or Watch Them Leave." McKinsey & Company, April 2021.

3. Gokalp, Yasemin (2019). "The Effects of Lean Six Sigma Training on Emotional Intelligence in a Large Corporation, Grand Canyon University." ProQuest, Dissertations Publishing, Ann Arbor, MI 27546297

4. Gallup research cited in McKinsey Individual Purpose survey, August 2020.

5. Bates, Dorton, Goldstrom & Mirza (2021). "Transformation in Uncertain Times: Tackling both the Urgent and the Important." McKinsey & Company, February 2021, 1-5

6. Harvard Business Review (2021). "On Change Management with J.P. Kotter."

7. Bryant & Sharer, "Are You Really Listening?" Harvard Business Review, 2021

8. Dobru, Hewes, Simon & Welchman, "Operating Model Transformations: Not all Elements are Created Equal." McKinsey & Company, September 2021

9. Buckingham & Goodall, "The Power of Hidden Teams." Published on HBR.org. May 2019, 3-7

10. Kahn, Komm, Maor & Pollner, "Back to Human: Why HR leaders want to focus on people again." McKinsey & Company, June 2021, 1-8

11. Hancock, Schaninger & Rahilly, "The Vanishing Middle Manager." McKinsey & Company. February 2021, 1-7

12. Goldsmith (2012), "Feedforward." Published online: marshallgoldsmithfeedforward.com

13. Huber & Sneader, "The Eight Trends that Will Define 2021 and Beyond." McKinsey & Company. June 2021, 1-6

14. Finn, Mysore, Usher & Brown, In Conversation: Managing in Extreme Uncertainty." McKinsey & Company. June 2021, 1-7

15. Fernandez-Araoz, Roscoe & Aramaki, "Turning Potential into Success— The Missing Link in Leadership Development." Harvard Business Review Magazine, November-December 2017, R1706E-PDF-ENG

16. Kahneman, Sibony, Fusaro & Sperling-Magro (2021). "Sounding the Alarm on System Noise." McKinsey Quarterly, May 2021

17. Oncken & Wass, Management Time: Who's Got the Monkey? Harvard Business Review, Magazine November-December 1999, R1706E-PDF-ENG

Chapter Two

1. Richard Higgins, Grace Liou, Susanne Maurenbrecher, Thomas Poppensieker, and Olivia White (2020). "Resilience, Strengthening Institutional Risk and Integrity." McKinsey & Company November 2020, 1-8

2. Julie Battilana, Tiziana Casciaro. "Don't Let Power Corrupt You." Harvard Business Review, September-October 2021.

3. Francesca Gino & Katherine Coffman. "Unconscious Bias, Training That Works." Harvard Business Review, September-October 2021.

4. The Adecco Group. "Disconnected Leaders: Bridging the Growing Chasm, Resetting Normal" 2021

5. Krivkovich & Levy (2015). "Managing the People Side of Risk." McKinsey & Company, May 2015, PDF-204KB

6. Rosabeth Moss Kanter. "Leadership for Change: Seven Enduring Skills for Experienced and Aspiring Change Leaders." Harvard Business School, Case Study, July 2020

7. Hancock et al. (2021).

8. Carucci (2021). "How Leaders Get in the Way of Organizational Change" Harvard Business School Publishing. Boston, MA

9. Boyatzis, Edmondson, Schaninger & De Smet (2020). "Psychological Safety, Emotional Intelligence and Leadership in a Time of Flux." McKinsey Quarterly. July 2020, PDF-578KB

10. Allas & Brady (2021). "The Boss Factor." McKinsey & Company, Podcast, April 27, 2021

11. O'Flaherty, Sanders & Whillans, "Research: A Little Recognition Can Provide a Big Morale Boost." Harvard Business Review, March 2021, H0695W-PDF-ENG

12. Cristancho, "3 Ways to Help Your Team Recover from Disruption." Harvard Business Review, April 2021, H069Z3-PDF-ENG

13. Buckingham, "What Great Managers Do." Harvard Business Review Magazine, March 2005, R0503D-PDF-ENG

14. Grant. "Persuading the Unpersuadable." Harvard Business Review Magazine, March-April 2021, R2102L-PDF-ENG

15. Thomas, Cooper, Cardazone, Urban, Bohrer, Long, Yee, Krivkovich, Huang, Prince, Kumar & Coury, "Women in the Workplace." McKinsey & Company, 2021

16. Hancock et al. (2021)

17. Hintsa (2021). "How Well-Being Improves Performance: An Interview with Annastiina Hintsa." McKinsey Quarterly, Interview, February 22, 2021

18. Segel (2021). "The Capability-Building Imperative: Make 'Purposeful Investments' in People." McKinsey & Company.

19. Bagheri, G., Zarei, R., & Aeen, M. N. (2012). Organizational silence (basic concepts and its development factors). Ideal Type of Management, 1(1), 47–58. Retrieved from https://www.researchgate.net/profile/Mojtaba_Nikaeen/publication/259383988_Organizational_Silence_Basic_Concepts_and_Its_Development_Factors/links/00463530707dcd18 4d000000.pdf

Chapter Three

1. Anicich & Hirsh (2017). "Why Being a Middle Manager Is So Exhausting." Harvard Business Review, March 2017, H03JR2-PDF-ENG

2. Chewning, McNally & Rutherford, "Lessons from the Military for COVID-Time Leadership." McKinsey & Company. May 2020, PDF-368KB

3. Goleman & Boyatzis (2008). "Social Intelligence and the Biology of Leadership." Harvard Business Review Magazine, September 2008, R0809E-PDF-ENG

4. Wiseman & McKeown (2010). Multipliers. Harper Collins, New York, NY

5. Benjamin Thomas and Kristen Lucas, Development and Validation of the Workplace Dignity Scale. Sage Journals 2018, pp. 72—103, https://doi.org/10.1177/1059601118807784

6. Ahmed, A., Liang, D., Anjum, M. A., & Durrani, D. K. (2021). Does dignity matter? The effects of workplace dignity on organization-based self-esteem and discretionary work effort. Current Psychology: A Journal for Diverse Perspectives on Diverse Psychological Issues. Advance online publication. https://doi.org/10.1007/s12144-021-01821-5

7. David & Congleton (2013). "Emotional Agility." Harvard Business Review, 2013, R1311L-PDF-ENG

8. Blomstrom (2021). "Psychological Safety." PeopleNotTech.

9. Gino & Coffman "Unconscious Bias Training that Works." Harvard Business Review Magazine. September-October 2021, R2105H-PDF-ENG

10. Fessell & Reivich (2021). "Why You Need to Protect Your Sense of Wonder—Especially Now." Harvard Business Review. August 2021, H06JG2-PDF-ENG

11. Kanter, et al (2020)

12. Allen & Aweh, "Inside DoorDash's Leadership Accelerator for Women of Color." Harvard Business Review, September 2021, H06JRB-PDF-ENG

13. Rock, Jones & Weller (2018). "Using Neuroscience to Make Feedback Work and Feel Better." Strategy + Business

14. DeFrancesco Soto & Mercedes "What We Lose when We Lose Women in the Workforce." McKinsey & Company, 2020

15. Cowden & Cummings (2011). "Nursing Theory and Concept Development: A Theoretical Model of Clinical Nurses' Intentions to Stay in Their Current Position. Journal of Advanced Nursing.

16. Hallowell (1998). "The Human Moment at Work." Harvard Business Review, January 1999, 99104-PDF-ENG

17. Toon W. Taris & Paul J.G. Schreurs (2009). "Well-Being and Organizational Performance: An Organizational-Level Test of the Happy-Productive Worker Hypothesis." Work & Stress, 23:2, pp. 120-136, DOI: 10.1080/02678370903072555.

Chapter Four

1. Ulrich & Smallwood (2004). "Capitalizing on Capabilities." Harvard Business Review OnPoint Collection, June 2004, 7014-PDF-ENG

2. Kaplan & Norton, "Measuring the Strategic Readiness of Intangible Assets." Harvard Business Review OnPoint Collection, February 2004, R0402C-PDF-ENG

3. Noureddin, L. Enabling Organizational Change: How First-level Managers Influence and Commit to Implementing and Sustaining Change in a Healthcare System, Dissertation, Grand Canyon University, 2018

4. Harvard Business Review (2021). On Change Management with J.P. Kotter, Harvard Business Review Publishing, Boston, MA

5. Campbell & Gavett (2021). "What Covid-19 Has Done to Our Well-Being, in 12 Charts." Harvard Business Review

6. Moss. "Beyond Burnout." Harvard Business Review, February 2021, BG2101-PDF-ENG

7. Lievens, "How the Pandemic Exacerbated Burnout." Harvard Business Review, February 2021, H066FF-PDF-ENG

8. Baugh & Raja, "Six Lessons on Fighting Burnout from Boston's Biggest Hospital." Harvard Business Review, February 2021, H066EN-PDF-ENG

9. DDI (2021). "Global Leadership Forecast."

10. Knight, "How to Help Your Team with Burnout When You're Burned Out Yourself." Harvard Business Review, March 2019, H04URE-PDF-ENG

11. Kramer (1983). "Reality Shock: Why Nurses Leave Nursing." AMACOM, American Management Association.

12. Liu, "How to Beat Loneliness and Make Friends." Harvard Business Review, February 2021, H066E3-PDF-ENG

13. Caldbeck (2021). "What I Learned when I Was Burned Out." Published on HRR.org.

14. Amy Cuddy, Matthew Kohut and John Neffinger, "Connect, Then Lead." Harvard Business Review Magazine, July-August 2013, R1307C-PDF-ENG

15. Buckingham & Goodall et al, (2020)

16. Jim Collins, Good to Great: Why Some Companies Make the Leap and Others Don't. New York: Harper Business, 2001, 11

17. Battilana & Casciaro, "Don't Let Power Corrupt You." Harvard Business Review, September—October 2021, R2105F-PDF-ENG

18. Fosslien, "What You're Getting Wrong about Burnout." MIT Sloan Management Review—August 2021, https://sloanreview.mit.edu/article/what-youre-getting-wrong-about-burnout

19. Marcus Buckingham and Curt Coffman (1999). First, Break All the Rules: What the World's Greatest Managers Do Differently. Simon & Schuster, New York, NY

20. Joanne Waldstreicher, "How Johnson & Johnson Made Hard Decisions during Covid." Harvard Business Review, June 2021, H06EIN-PDF-ENG

21. Courtney, Lovallo & Clarke, "Deciding How to Decide." Harvard Business Review, December 2013, https://hbr.org/webinar/2014/01/deciding-how-to-decide

22. Michael T. Ford, Christopher P. Cerasoli, Jennifer A. Higgins & Andrew L. Decesare (2011). "Relationships between Psychological, Physical, and Behavioral Health and Work Performance: A Review and Meta-analysis." Work & Stress, 25:3, pp. 185-204, DOI: 10.1080/02678373.2011.609035.

23. Peter Cappelli, "How Financial Accounting Screws Up HR" Harvard Business Review Magazine, January-February 2023, HBR Reprint S23011

24. Amy Gallo, "How to Navigate Conflict with a Coworker." Harvard Business Review Magazine September-October 2022, adapted from "Getting Along: How to Work with Anyone (Even Difficult People)", (Harvard Business Review Press, 2022

25. Heidi K. Gardner and Ivan Matviak, "Performance Management Shouldn't Kill Collaboration.", Harvard Business Review Magazine September-October 2022

26. Elizabeth Heichler, "Good Questions", MIT Sloan Management Review, Winter 2024 Issue

27. Microsoft Work Trend Index Special Report, "Hybrid Work is Just Work. Are We Doing It Wrong?", September 22, 2022, https://www.microsoft.com/en-us/worklab/work-trend-index/hybrid-work-is-just-work

28. Cian McEnroe and David Rock, "3 Ways Our Brains Undermine Our Ability to Be a Good Leader.", Harvard Business Review, July 2023, H07QBV-PDF-ENG

29. Michael Birshan and Ishaan Seth, "How ambidextrous leaders manage through volatile times", McKinsey & Company, January 2023/Podcast

30. Dina Denham Smith, "When Your Boss Gives You a Totally Unrealistic Goal", Harvard Business Review, January 2024

31. David Brooks, *How to Know a Person: The Art of Seeing Others Deeply and Being Deeply Seen,* Random House Publishing Group. Kindle Edition, 2024

Chapter Five

1. Noureddin, L. Enabling Organizational Change: How First-level Managers Influence and Commit to Implementing and Sustaining Change in a Healthcare System, Dissertation, Grand Canyon University, 2018

2. Kaplan & McMillan (2021). "Reimagining the Balanced Scorecard for the ESG Era." Harvard Business Review, February 2021, H0609P-PDF-ENG

3. Collins & Porras, "Building Your Company's Vision." Harvard Business Review Magazine, September—October 1996, 96501-PDF-ENG

4. Claman (2021). "Set Better Boundaries." Harvard Business Review, January 2021, H063ME-PDF-ENG

5. Dubey, (2016) "What Google Learned from Its Quest to Build the Perfect Team." New York Times Magazine, p. 20

6. Rogers & Blenko, "Who Has the D? How Clear Decision Roles Enhance Organizational Performance." Harvard Business Review Magazine, January 2006, R0601D-PDF-ENG

7. Blomstrom (2021). "People Before Tech: Psychological Safety and Teamwork in the Digital Age." PeopleNotTech.

8. Markman, "How to Have Difficult Conversations Virtually." Harvard Business Review, July 2019, H051DX-PDF-ENG

9. Gallo, "Managing People on a Sinking Ship." Harvard Business Review. November 2013, H00K4P-PDF-ENG

10. Hooijberg & Watkins (2021). "The Future of Team Leadership is Multimodal." MIT Sloan Management Review, February 2021, R62324

11. Bourke & Espedido (2020). "The Key to Inclusive Leadership." Harvard Business Review, March 2020, H05GLB-PDF-ENG

12. Gokalp (2019). "The Effects of Lean Six Sigma Training on Emotional Intelligence in a Large Corporation, Grand Canyon University." ProQuest Dissertations Publishing, 27546297.

Chapter Six

1. Blomstrom (2021). "People Before Tech: Psychological Safety and Teamwork in the Digital Age." PeopleNotTech.

2. Liz Wiseman (2016). "Multipliers, Revised and Updated: How the Best Leaders Make Everyone Smarter." Harper Collins Publishers

3. Donald Sull and Charles Sull (2021). "10 Things Your Culture Needs to Get Right." MIT Sloan Management Review. 63211

4. Gardner and Matviak (2022). "Performance Management Shouldn't Kill Collaboration." Harvard Business Review Magazine. September-October

5. Gallo (2022). "How to Navigate Conflict with a Coworker." Harvard Business Review Magazine September-October

6. Bailey (2023). "A Two-Minute Burnout Checkup." Harvard Business Review Digital Article

7. McEnroe and Rock (2023). "3 Ways Our Brains Undermine Our Ability to Be a

Good Leader." Harvard Business Review Digital Article. H07QBV-PDF-ENG

8. Heifetz and Linsky (2002). "A Survival Guide for Leaders." Harvard Business Review Magazine June. R0206C-PDF-ENG

9. Baugh and Raja (2021). "Six Lessons on Fighting Burnout from Boston's Biggest Hospital." Harvard Business Review, H066EN-PDF-ENG

10. Moss (2021). "The Burnout Crisis." Harvard Business Review." BG2101-PDF-ENG

11. Leschke-Kahle (2024). "What We're Still Getting Wrong About Performance Management." MIT Sloan Management Review

12. Buckingham (2021). "The Top 10 Findings on Resilience and Engagement." MIT Sloan Management Review

13. Brassey, Herbig, Jeffery, and Ungerman (2023). "Reframing employee health: Moving beyond burnout to holistic health." McKinsey Health Institute

Chapter Seven

1. Maber (2024). "The future of work depends on understanding Gen Alpha" Fast Company, The Future of Work Newsletter, 91023970

2. Gallo (2022). "How to Navigate Conflict with a Coworker." Harvard Business Review Magazine September-October

3. Michael Birshan and Ishaan Seth, "How ambidextrous leaders manage through volatile times", McKinsey & Company, January 2023/Podcast

4. Dina Denham Smith, "When Your Boss Gives You a Totally Unrealistic Goal", Harvard Business Review, January 2024

5. Te Wu and Ram Misra (2024), "Why Big Projects Fail—and How to Give Yours a Better Chance of Success." Harvard Business Review, H07VLV-PDF-ENG

6. N. Anand and Jean-Louis Barsoux (2023), "Fixing a Self-Sabotaging Team." Harvard Business Review Magazine March-April, R2302J-PDF-ENG

7. Adi Ignatius (2024), "Why It's So Hard to Get Things Done.", Harvard Business Review Magazine January-February

8. Korn Ferry (2022). "Whiplash Leadership." Korn Ferry Briefings Issue 52

9. Miles (2022). "Revisiting Project Oxygen: A look at what makes a good manager." BetterUp Article, Project Oxygen

10. Katzenback, Giacoman and Morley-Fletcher (2020), "Why authentic informal leaders are key to an organization's emotional health." Strategy+Business, PWC Publication

11. Noureddin, L. Enabling Organizational Change: How First-level Managers Influence and Commit to Implementing and Sustaining Change in a Healthcare System, Dissertation, Grand Canyon University, 2018

12. Gokalp (2019). "The Effects of Lean Six Sigma Training on Emotional Intelligence in a Large Corporation, Grand Canyon University." ProQuest Dissertations Publishing, 27546297.

13. Brown, Mani, Sheppard and Wakefeld (2024), "Transformative Leadership for Extraordinary Times", Strategy-Business, PwC Publication

14. Maqbool, R., Sudong, Y., Manzoor, N., & Rashid, Y. (2017). The impact of emotional intelligence, project managers' competencies, and transformational leadership on project success: An empirical perspective. Project Management Journal, 48(3), 58-75. doi:10.1177/875697281704800304

Chapter Eight

1. Noureddin, L. Enabling Organizational Change: How First-level Managers Influence and Commit to Implementing and Sustaining Change in a Healthcare System, Dissertation, Grand Canyon University, 2018

2. Miles (2022). "Revisiting Project Oxygen: A look at what makes a good manager." BetterUp Article, Project Oxygen

3. Dhingra, Samo, Schaninger and Schrimper (2021). "Help your employees find purpose or watch them leave", McKinsey & Company, Organization Practice

4. Brown, Mani, Sheppard and Wakefeld (2024), "Transformative Leadership for Extraordinary Times", Strategy-Business, PwC Publication

About the Authors

Loubna Noureddin, Ed.D, Master Certified Coach

How do we inspire people to lead through humanity? That is the question that has haunted Dr. Loubna since her childhood experience with not one, but two civil wars, in Sierra Leone and Lebanon.

Loubna has devoted her work to understanding the behaviors of leaders and teams with an unwavering passion to influence people to choose peace, not war, with themselves, their teams, and the organizations they support.

In 2006, Loubna stumbled upon the power of driving human change through a combination of teaching, experimenting, and purpose-driven coaching conversations. As a thought leader in organizational leadership and culture, Loubna brings a unique global perspective and extensive experience in healthcare, higher education, not-for-profit, and technology industries.

Loubna spent the last two decades serving organizations by fostering leaders and their teams for success. Her leadership programs were rated among the top ten in the globe by *Training Magazine*. She worked with *Harvard ManageMentor* to design customized training programs for healthcare leaders. She is a contributor to *Forbes* and a frequent speaker and facilitator for local and global organizations.

Loubna is the Co-Founder and CEO of Mind Market, a consulting firm dedicated to helping organizations create a constant stream of leaders who can tackle any challenge. She supports executives in leading change through a deeper understanding of influence, team behaviors, and culture dynamics.

In her spare time, Loubna enjoys nature photography and builds on her dream to support 100 orphans from West Africa through career transitions. She is a proud mother of two amazing daughters, and resides in Miami, FL with her life-long friend and husband.

Suzie Hise

Suzie Hise is a leadership development and change management consultant with over 30 years of experience in operations, strategic planning, and leadership training. Drawing on her extensive background in corporate, health-care, education, governance, and public sectors, she provides targeted executive coaching and training to individuals, teams, and organizations to help them navigate through times of profound change.

Suzie brings national and international expertise on performance analytics to support development of programs based on empowering leaders and their teams to unlock their own potential for growth. Her career history of creating opportunities in the face of adversity enables her to teach and mentor from a place of compassion and empathy.

She has served as an executive coach for physicians at Nicklaus Children's Health System and a leadership coach at Miami Children's Health Foundation. Suzie's previous roles include Senior Vice President of Strategy and Development for Gibraltar Private Bank & Trust, Director of Service and Training for Kelly Services, Inc., and executive coach for senior executives and lead scientists at Andrx Pharmaceuticals and Biotest Pharmaceuticals. Suzie has also advised the University of Miami and the Governor of Michigan and served on the Advisory Board for the Michigan State Board of Education.

Suzie loves exploring art fairs, joining community events and taking leisurely walks with her friends in beautiful Miami.